A Troubleshooting Guide for Writers

STRATEGIES AND PROCESS

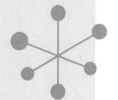

Fourth Edition

A Troubleshooting Guide for Writers

STRATEGIES AND PROCESS

Barbara Fine Clouse

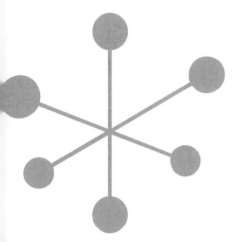

Boston   Burr Ridge, IL   Dubuque, IA   Madison, WI   New York
San Francisco   St. Louis   Bangkok   Bogotá   Caracas   Kuala Lumpur
Lisbon   London   Madrid   Mexico City   Milan   Montreal   New Delhi
Santiago   Seoul   Singapore   Sydney   Taipei   Toronto

Higher Education

A TROUBLESHOOTING GUIDE FOR WRITERS: STRATEGIES AND PROCESS
Published by McGraw-Hill, a business unit of the McGraw-Hill Companies, Inc., 1221 Avenue of the Americas, New York, NY, 10020. Copyright © 2005, 2001, 1997, 1993, by The McGraw-Hill Companies, Inc. All rights reserved. No part of this publication may be reproduced or distributed in any form or by any means, or stored in a database or retrieval system, without the prior written consent of The McGraw-Hill Companies, Inc., including, but not limited to, in any network or other electronic storage or transmission, or broadcast for distance learning.
Some ancillaries, including electronic and print components, may not be available to customers outside the United States.

This book is printed on acid-free paper.

1 2 3 4 5 6 7 8 9 0 FGR/FGR 0 9 8 7 6 5 4

ISBN 0-07-287689-1

President of McGraw-Hill Humanities/Social Sciences: *Steve Debow*
Publisher: *Lisa Moore*
Sponsoring editor: *Christopher Bennem*
Developmental editor: *Anne Stameshkin*
Executive marketing manager: *David S. Patterson*
Senior media producer: *Todd Vaccaro*
Project manager: *Ruth Smith*
Production supervisor: *Janean A. Utley*
Associate designer: *Srdj Savanovic*
Lead supplement producer: *Marc Mattson*
Cover design: *Srdj Savanovic*
Interior design: *Ellen Pettengell*
Typeface: *10/12 Meridien Roman*
Compositor: *Shepherd, Inc.*
Printer: *Quebecor World Fairfield Inc.*

Library of Congress Cataloging-in-Publication Data
Clouse, Barbara Fine.
    A troubleshooting guide for writers: strategies and process / Barbara Fine Clouse.—4th ed.
        p. cm.
    Includes index.
    ISBN 0-07-287689-1 (acid-free paper)
    1. English language—Rhetoric. 2. English language—Grammar. 3. Report writing. I.
Title.
PE1408.C5378 2005
808'.042—dc22   2003068635

For Jeremy, Brady, and Julia
and
In loving memory of Bob Krantz

Table of contents

PART III

A Troubleshooting Guide to Revising 71

Preface

A Troubleshooting Guide for Writers: Strategies and Process is a compendium of strategies for handling all aspects of writing, from idea generation through editing. It is based on the belief that people write better when they discover procedures that work well for them.

GOALS

The many writing strategies in *A Troubleshooting Guide for Writers* serve two important purposes:

- To provide a range of strategies for writers to sample as they work to develop successful writing processes
- To help writers when they get stuck by providing specific strategies for solving writing problems

WHY A NEW TITLE?

In its first three editions, this book was titled *Working It Out: A Troubleshooting Guide for Writers.* The approach and scope of the book remain the same; the new title better reflects the book's goals: to help students solve writing problems and to help them improve their writing processes.

FEATURES

The features of *A Troubleshooting Guide for Writers* aim to make the book an efficient reference for those who want to improve their writing processes by discovering effective procedures and by developing successful problem-solving strategies.

New Over 284 Helpful Strategies

Over 40 strategies have been added! With so many helpful procedures described, all users should find ways to solve problems and improve their writing processes.

Clear, Jargon-Free Prose Written in a Conversational Style

So the book can be a ready reference both in and out of the classroom, explanations are concise and written in a supportive, nonintimidating style.

Organization across the Writing Process

Writers can use the text in the same sequence as their writing. Part I treats prewriting; Part II treats drafting; Part III treats revising; Part IV treats editing.

Chapters Structured as Responses to Questions and Comments Voiced by Student Writers

Students can find what they need faster because chapter titles echo their own language and concerns.

An Overview of the Writing Process and Essay Structure

The Introduction contains information on the stages of the writing process, audience, purpose, and essay structure.

New A Focus on Collaboration

Chapter 11 offers strategies to help students incorporate peer review into their revision processes.

New Illustrations of Revising

Each of the chapters in Part III (A Troubleshooting Guide to Revising) includes an "Examining a Draft" section that uses a student essay to illustrate the revising process.

New Strategies for Incorporating Research

Part V focuses on finding and using source material. An annotated student paper using research illustrates the points made in this section.

Revised A Greater Emphasis on Composing with a Computer

Frequently occurring "Troubleshooting with a Computer" sections offer strategies for those who compose at the computer. Each of these sections also includes helpful websites.

Useful Appendixes

Appendix A contains 15 ideas for writing, in rhetorical context. Appendix B describes strategies for writing essay examination answers.

New and Revised Additional Coverage

Chapter 3 has been expanded to include information on informal outlining, Chapter 18 includes more information on eliminating sentence fragments, and Chapter 21 includes strategies for using verb tenses correctly. A new chapter—Chapter 26—covers strategies for capitalizing.

A NOTE TO STUDENTS

Pretend for a moment that you play tennis and that you are having trouble with your baseline shots. A coach, noticing your problem, might suggest that you drop your hip a little. Now pretend that you are a runner and you are having trouble improving your time in the 1,600-meter race. In this case, your coach might suggest that you swing your arms more and pretend a giant hand is on your back pushing you along. That's what coaches do: They make suggestions to help you solve problems that arise as a natural part of learning to do something better.

As you work to become a better writer, think of this book as one of your coaches. If you encounter a problem, look to this book for one or more suggestions for solving that problem.

HERE'S HOW TO USE THIS BOOK FOR BEST RESULTS.

- Read over the table of contents so you know what this book covers. Notice that most of the chapters are titled with a remark often spoken by a struggling writer.

- If you get stuck, return to the table of contents and find the remark that best expresses the problem you are having. Turn to the chapter titled with that remark.

- Quickly read the chapter (it will be short). Several strategies for solving your writing problem will be explained. Select one of the strategies and give it a try. If it works, great. If not, try another—and another until you solve your problem. (If none of the procedures works, speak to your instructor or writing center tutor.)
- If you are not having any problems but want to discover more effective or efficient procedures, read through the book and mark the procedures to try the next time you write.

Of course, this book is not your only coach. Your classroom teacher is the best coach of all, and your classmates and the tutors in the writing center are also good sources of information. So if you have a problem, you can also talk to one of these people to get suggestions for a overcoming the obstacle. Ask them what specific procedures they follow, and try some of them to see if they work well for you too.

Acknowledgments

I am grateful to Lisa Moore, Anne Stameshkin, and Ruth Smith of McGraw-Hill for their support and expert guidance. In addition, I owe much to the sound counsel of the following reviewers, whose insights inform this book:

Steven E. Cohen, Norwalk Community College
Donald Erskine, Clark College
Lahcen Elyazghi Ezzaher, University Of Northern Colorado
Carol S. Manning, Mary Washington College
Sue McIntyre, Humboldt State University
Robbi Nester, Irvine Valley College
Deborah Coxwell Teague, Florida State University
Julie Whitlow, Salem State College

Finally, to my understanding husband, Denny, and to my children, Greg and Jeff, I offer thanks for the support and for the room of my own.

Myths about Writing

AN INTRODUCTION

People say many things about writing. Some of what they say is true, and some is not. Can you tell the difference?

Which of the following statements are facts, and which are myths? (The next section will supply the answers, but don't peek.)

Writers are born, not made.

"Good" writers write fast.

Writers should wait for inspiration.

"Good" writers rarely struggle.

"Good" writers get it right the first time.

Outlining is very time-consuming.

The longer the words, the better they are.

Revising is reading over a draft and
fixing spelling and punctuation.

After drafting, "good" writers look for
their grammar mistakes right away.

There is only one way to write.

An essay has no identifiable parts.

Introductions should be written first.

A well-stated point does not require proof.

After making their last point, writes should just stop.

Sentence fragments are always short.

Run-ons and comma splices are always long.

Use a comma wherever you pause in speech.

Capitalize a word to emphasize it.

There are no rules to explain English spelling.

The longer the writing, the better it is.

Don't Believe Everything You Hear

Much of what you hear about writing just isn't true, including the statements in the box above—every one of those statements is a common myth about writing. If you are surprised to learn that these statements are untrue, read the chapters indicated below for accurate information.

Myth	Accurate Information
Writers are born, not made.	Introduction
"Good" writers write fast.	Chapters 9–16
Writers should wait for inspiration.	Chapter 1
"Good" writers rarely struggle.	Introduction
"Good" writers get it right the first time.	Chapters 4–16
Outlining is very time-consuming.	Chapter 3
The longer the words, the better they are.	Chapter 8
Revising is reading over a draft and fixing spelling and punctuation.	Chapters 10–11
After drafting, "good" writers look for their grammar mistakes right away.	Introduction
There is only one way to write.	Chapters 1–16
An essay has no identifiable parts.	Introduction
Introductions should be written first.	Chapter 5

❋ How to Become a Better Writer

MYTH: *Writers are born, not made.*

"I'm a terrible writer." Instructors hear students say that all the time, and maybe you have said it yourself. If so, you are probably wrong. More likely, you are not as good a writer as you could be—or would like to be—but now you have the chance to become a better writer, even an excellent one.

Maybe you think you can't be a good writer because you weren't *born* a good writer. Again, you are mistaken, for you can *learn* to be a good writer. Becoming a better writer has much in common with becoming a better swimmer, piano player, or dancer. In all these cases, you can work to improve a skill. As you work to improve your writing skills, think about the following habits of highly successful writers.

7 HABITS OF HIGHLY SUCCESSFUL WRITERS

1. **Be patient.** Improving a skill takes time. Just as perfecting a foul shot takes a basketball player time and practice, so too does improving your writing. If you expect too much too soon, you will become frustrated. Look for slow, steady progress rather than dramatic, overnight improvement.

2. **Expect to get stuck.** Everyone does, even experienced, professional writers. Writer's block and dead ends are all part of writing, so do not think there is something wrong with you if you have some trouble. Consult this text, your instructor, other experienced writers, and/or a writing center tutor when you get stuck. When you solve the problem, tuck the solution away for future reference, so the same problem does not plague you over and over again.

3. **Remember that writing is really rewriting.** Experienced writers work and rework drafts several times. With each revision, know that you are acting like an experienced writer.

4. **Talk to other writers.** Find out what they do when they write, and try some of their procedures. Form a network with your classmates and other writers for support and suggestions.

5. **Study the responses to your writing.** What does your instructor say about your writing? What do your classmates say when they read your drafts? What do people in the writing center say? Reader response is valuable to a writer. By paying attention to this response and working to improve areas where readers see weaknesses, you can improve more quickly. If you do not understand a response or if you do not know how to make a change, ask for help.

6. **Read, read, read.** Read every day—the newspaper, news-magazines, short stories, crime novels. Read anything that interests you. Notice how other writers handle introductions, conclusions, supporting detail, and transitions. Look up unfamiliar words, notice sentence structure, and observe punctuation. The more you read, the more you learn about the nature of language, and the faster your writing will improve. Furthermore, frequent reading makes you more knowledgeable, so you have more ideas for your writing.

7. **Do not fear mistakes.** They are a natural part of learning. Take risks; try things out. If you make mistakes, embrace them as opportunities to learn. If you are afraid of making a mistake, you will never try; if you never try, you will never grow. Connect your mistakes to your writing procedures. Decide which procedures work well for you and which do not. Then consult this text and your instructor for procedures to replace ones that did not work. For example, maybe idea generation goes well for you, but revision does not. That means you need to discover new revision procedures. When your procedures work better, your writing will improve.

Understand That Writing Is a Process

> **MYTH:** "Good" writers write fast.

Very few worthwhile endeavors are accomplished quickly, and writing is no different. Successful writers typically engage in a number of activities, and doing so takes time. These activities are

1. Prewriting
2. Drafting
3. Revising
4. Editing

Writers do not always move in a straight line from prewriting to drafting to revising to editing. Instead, they often double back before going forward. For example, while drafting you may think of a new idea to add, so you have left drafting and doubled back to prewriting. While editing, you may think of a better way to phrase an idea, so you have left editing and doubled back to revising. Never consider any stage of the process "done" and behind you. Always stand ready to return to an earlier stage when a good idea strikes you.

Now let's consider what each stage of writing involves.

Prewriting

> **MYTH**: Writers should wait for inspiration.

If you sit around waiting for inspiration, you may never get anything written; inspiration does not occur often enough for writers to depend on it. In fact, inspiration occurs so rarely that writers must develop other ways to get ideas. Collectively, the procedures for coming up with ideas in the absence of inspiration are called **prewriting.** The term *prewriting* is used because these procedures come before writing the first draft.

Chapters 1–3 describe procedures for coming up with ideas to write about and for discovering ways to order those ideas.

Drafting

> **MYTH**: "Good" writers get it right the first time.

Once writers generate enough ideas during prewriting to serve as a departure point, they make their first attempt at getting those ideas down. This part of the writing process is **drafting.** Typically, the first draft is very rough, which is why it so often is called the **rough draft.** The rough draft provides raw material that can be shaped and refined in the next stages of the writing process.

Chapters 4–8 describe drafting procedures.

Revising

> **MYTH**: Revising is reading over a draft and fixing spelling and punctuation.

During **revising** writers rework the raw material of the draft to get it in shape. This reworking is a time-consuming, difficult part of the process. It requires the writer to refine the content so that it is clear, so that points are adequately supported, and so that ideas are expressed in the best way possible and in the best order possible.

Chapters 9–16 describe revising procedures.

Editing

> **MYTH**: After drafting, "good" writers look for their grammar mistakes right away.

Because experienced readers expect your writing to be free of errors, you must **edit** to find and eliminate mistakes so that they do not distract or annoy your reader. However, many writers hunt for errors too soon, before they have revised for content and effective expression. Editing should really be saved for the end of the process.

Chapters 17–27 describe editing procedures.

Develop Your Own Writing Process

> **MYTH**: There is only one way to write.

Although we have been discussing "the" writing process, there really is no single, correct process. Instead, writers develop procedures that work well for them, so that every successful writer can have a different, successful process. As you use this book and work to become a better writer, try different procedures for prewriting, drafting, revising, and editing. Some of these procedures will work well for you and some will not. Continue sampling until you have effective strategies for handling all the stages of writing, and at that point you will have discovered your own successful process.

Be Aware of Your Purpose

Everything you write has a purpose. Even something as simple as a grocery list is written for a purpose: to make sure you don't forget to buy everything you need. The fact is, if you don't have a reason for writing, why bother?

Four common purposes for writing are

- To relate experience
- To inform
- To persuade
- To entertain

The first reason for writing is to **relate experience,** perhaps to express your feelings about the experience or reflect upon it. For example, if you interviewed to be a lab assistant in the biology department, afterwards you might write a friend an e-mail about the experience and how nervous you were. People enjoy sharing experience because it helps them connect with others. You might also write in your journal to reflect on what happened and evaluate your interview. Such written reflection is valuable as a way to understand events.

Another reason for writing is to **inform,** perhaps to increase the reader's knowledge, establish a record, or provide help. For example, a magazine article about cholesterol can increase a reader's understanding of how this substance affects the body. The proceedings of government agencies recorded into documents serve as a permanent history. The owner's manual for a DVD player explains how to operate the device, so the owner can use it properly. We need informational writing to communicate important knowledge with others and to preserve significant facts.

A third reason for writing is to **persuade** a reader to think or act a particular way. For example, you might write a letter to the editor of your campus newspaper to convince students to vote for a particular student government candidate. Or you might write a letter to convince a store manager to refund your money for a defective product you purchased. People are always trying to influence each other, and persuasive writing is one way they exert that influence.

The last reason for writing is to **entertain.** Short stories, romance novels, and humorous newspaper columns, for example, are written to entertain. Without such creative writing, we would lose an important pleasure, and our lives would be diminished.

Finally, writers often combine purposes. For example, you might write a description of your favorite fishing spot both to share your fishing experience there <u>and</u> entertain your reader.

You must be aware of your purpose for writing because purpose affects what you write and how you write it. Say you are writing about discovering mice in the apartment you just rented. Notice how different the writings become when your purpose changes:

To share experience The writing might tell how upset you are about the discovery of the mice.

To inform The writing might explain what happens when a dwelling has mice in it, or it could explain how one rids a dwelling of mice.

To persuade The writing might give reasons your landlord should refund your rent and deposit because of the mice, or it might give reasons why people should have apartments inspected before signing a rental contract.

To entertain The writing might be a funny story about what it is like living with mice.

Think about Your Reader

Your **audience** (the person or people who will read your writing) affects what you say and how you say it. For example, say that you need to borrow $100 to get through the month because you did not live within your budget. If you were e-mailing a close friend to request the loan, your writing would be relaxed and informal. You might not even explain why you have come up short or when you will repay the money. Your writing might be something like this:

To...	Frazier, Dale
Cc...	
Subject:	help!

Hey, Dale –

I hate to do this to you, but I need a hundred bucks fast – never mind why. I'll get it back to you as soon as I can.

Lee

If you were writing a note to your parents, you would be a little more formal and forthcoming about why you need the money and how you will pay it back:

My phone bill was higher than I expected, so I'm short of money this month. I'm really sorry—I've learned my lesson about calling Jan every day. I plan to work overtime three days next week, so I know I can repay the loan after my next paycheck.

Now consider a letter asking your boss to advance you $100. For this audience, your writing would be the most formal of all. It could look like the letter on p. 9.

As you can see, your reader's situation affects what you write. For example, assume you are writing to convince your reader that a longer school year is a good idea. If your audience includes working mothers, you might mention that a longer school year will cut down on child-care hassles. However, if your audience includes teenagers, this argument would mean little. Instead, you might note that they would be more competitive when they apply for admission into college.

One way to gear your writing to your audience is to complete a reader profile like the one explained on pages 78–79.

NOTE: Perhaps you are thinking that if you are in a writing class your audience will be your writing instructor. Keep in mind, however, that writing teachers can assume the identities of different audiences so you can practice writing for a range of readers.

450 Granada Avenue
Truesdale, OH 44512
January 14, 2004

Ms. Marian Mattura, General Manager
The Campus Diner
88501 Lane Avenue
Truesdale, OH 44520

Dear Ms. Mattura:

I wish to request a $100 advance on my salary for next month. I hope the fact that I have been a reliable employee at the Campus Diner for two years and the fact that I have never asked for an advance in the past will persuade you to grant my request.

Ms. Mattura, I am already scheduled to work overtime three days next week, so I am certain I will have no trouble repaying this loan. I am also certain I will never need to ask for an advance again, because I now understand the importance of sticking to a budget.

Thank you very much for considering my request.

Sincerely,

Dale

Dale Frazier

TEST YOURSELF: Find the Intersection of Audience and Purpose

Two pieces of writing that have the same purpose will be very different if written for different audiences. Consider the recruitment letters sent out by your college admissions office. A letter aimed at recruiting a star high school athlete may highlight one aspect of your college, while a letter aimed at a prospective theater major may highlight a different aspect. Similarly, pieces written for the same audience but with different purposes will also be different. Consider two letters sent out by your school's alumni office to recent graduates. A letter inviting the graduates to join the alumni association will be very different from one urging the graduates to make a contribution to the school.

Three Writing Tasks Assume that you borrowed your brother's car and that while it was parked someone sideswiped it, causing extensive damage. Now assume you have three writing tasks ahead of you:

1. Leaving your brother a note explaining what happened to the car.
2. Writing your parents to explain what happened so you can borrow money to have the car fixed.
3. Writing your friend who attends another school to tell that person what happened.

How will these three pieces of writing differ? How will the audience and purpose be responsible for those differences?

Know What an Essay Is

MYTH: An essay has no identifiable parts.

Pause for a moment and think about the forms people use for their writing: letters, memos, diary and journal entries, e-mail, web pages, message board postings, chat room forums, lab reports, book reports, résumés, newspaper and magazine articles, editorials, advertisements, brochures, even flyers tacked up on telephone poles—and that's not all of them. In college, however, the most frequently used form is the **essay**—a brief writing composed of several paragraphs, all relating to a single topic. In general, an essay has three parts:

- The introduction
- The body paragraphs
- The conclusion

The Introduction

MYTH: Introductions should be written first.

The opening paragraph or paragraphs of an essay are the **introduction.** The introduction is important because it must create interest in the essay so readers want to read on. Have you ever started a magazine article, read a paragraph or so, and moved on to another article without finishing? If so, the introduction failed to stimulate your interest. Don't worry about writing your introduction before the rest of your paper. Sometimes the best introductions are written last.

Chapter 5 explains strategies for writing introductions that stimulate reader interest.

The Thesis

In addition to creating interest in the essay, the introduction often includes a **thesis,** which is the statement of the essay's topic and the writer's assertion about that topic, like this:

Thesis: Network news broadcasts do not adequately inform the public.

Essay's topic: Network news broadcasts

Writer's assertion: They do an inadequate job of informing the public.

A good thesis presents an idea worth writing about—something disputed or in need of explanation.

Acceptable thesis: Although everyone agrees that children must be adequately cared for, this country does not properly regulate day-care centers.

Explanation: The thesis idea is debatable and in need of explanation.

Unacceptable thesis: Children must be adequately cared for.

Explanation: No one will disagree with the thesis idea, so why bother writing about it?

Acceptable thesis: Rose Lewin, my grandmother, is a woman of courage and determination.

Explanation: The thesis idea requires explanation.

Unacceptable thesis: Rose Lewin is my grandmother.

Explanation: The thesis idea is a statement of fact that requires no explanation and needs no debate.

Chapter 2 explains strategies for writing acceptable thesis statements.

To give you an idea of how an introduction can stimulate interest and present the thesis, here is an introduction taken from the essay on page 16.

Writer stimulates interest with a list of problems in schools, a warning about the complexity of the issue, and a brief summary of her assertion.	Right now, something is terribly wrong in our public schools: test scores are down, attendance is dropping, violence is increasing, students are bored and angst-ridden, teachers are demoralized, and parents are frustrated, angry, and worried. Because the problems are multifaceted, the solutions are likely to be complex. However, many are still looking to the quick fix, in this case wearing school uniforms. Uniforms have long been worn by students in private schools, but lately more people are calling for them in public schools. Advocates claim that uniforms will solve everything from low self-esteem and poor grades to minor discipline problems and outbursts of serious violence. When pressed to back up their claims, however, the advocates can do little more than cite anecdotal evidence, because there is no proof that uniforms accomplish all that some say they do. <u>In fact, requiring public school students to wear uniforms will create a new set of problems.</u>
The thesis is underlined as a study aid.	

The Body Paragraphs

> **MYTH**: A well-stated point does not require proof.

Do you believe everything you read? Of course not, and your audience doesn't either. That's why your reader will not believe your thesis is true unless you *prove* that it is. Does your thesis state that schools should teach conflict resolution? Then you have to provide solid reasons why this is a good idea. Does your thesis state that high-protein weight-loss diets can be dangerous? Then you must explain how the diets can be harmful. Does your thesis state that the new education building is an eyesore? Then you need to describe the unattractive features of the building. And that is where the body paragraphs come in. The **body paragraphs** present the ideas that prove or explain your thesis so your reader will accept its truth.

Body paragraphs typically have two parts:

- The topic sentence
- The supporting details

The **topic sentence** tells what point the paragraph makes to prove or explain the thesis. The **supporting details** are all the ideas that develop the topic sentence's point. To help you recognize the two parts of a body paragraph, examine these two body paragraphs, written to prove or explain the thesis, "In fact, requiring public school students to wear uniforms will create a new set of problems." (The topic sentences are underlined as a study aid.)

The supporting details develop the point stated in the topic sentence.

> Unlike private schools, public schools cannot require students to wear uniforms. Certainly, public schools can establish and enforce reasonable dress codes, but because the Constitution guarantees everyone's right to a public education, those who object to wearing uniforms for religious or other compelling reasons cannot be kept out of school. This means that public schools can do little more than *urge* students to wear uniforms. If many choose not to, what is accomplished? If some students wear uniforms and others do not, the chances are good that the two groups of students will be treated differently by teachers and administrators. They will likely give preferential treatment to those who wear the recommended uniforms. After all, these are the students that teachers and administrators favor, the ones who do as they are told. Those who choose not to wear uniforms can easily become second-class citizens because they will be perceived as the trouble-makers, as the ones who do not follow the rules. <u>Thus, uniforms in public schools are likely to create a two-tiered caste system and promote preferential treatment.</u>

Each topic sentence presents one point to explain or prove the thesis.

The supporting details develop the point stated in the topic sentence.

<u>Perhaps more important is the fact that a school-uniform policy eliminates opportunity for self-expression.</u> The elimination of self-expression is worrisome because school already demands so much conformity: everyone takes the same classes, keeps the same hours, chooses from the same activities, behaves according to the same rules, and learns the same material. School should help young people express their individuality and creativity so they become comfortable with their personal styles and learn to appreciate the differences around them, but how can they do that if everything about the institution calls for conformity? Allowing students to choose what to wear affords them a harmless respite from the conformity inherent in so much of public education.

The Topic Sentence

Often, as the second body paragraph above illustrates, the topic sentence comes at or near the beginning of the paragraph. Sometimes, as the first body paragraph above illustrates, the topic sentence comes at or near the end of the paragraph. When you place the topic sentence first or nearly first, you give your reader an upfront statement of the point you will develop in support of the thesis, and then you go on to provide supporting details to prove that point. When you place your topic sentence last or nearly last, your supporting details provide specific evidence that leads to the conclusion stated in the topic sentence.

Sometimes the topic sentence is not stated at all. Instead, it is strongly implied by the supporting details. When the topic sentence is implied, readers must use the clues in the body paragraph to determine what point is being made to explain or prove the thesis. Here is an example of a body paragraph with an implied topic sentence. As you read, determine what point is being made to support the thesis, "In fact, requiring public school students to wear uniforms will create a new set of problems."

Proponents of school uniforms say that uniforms reduce gang influence, that they minimize violence by reducing some of the sources of conflict among students, and that they help identify those who are trespassing on school property. It is true that gang affiliation can be signaled by clothing and that students have been attacked because of what they wear. However, uniforms will not necessarily address this problem because students are still free to wear jewelry, watches, shoes, and coats for which they can be the targets of violence. They can also carry backpacks, ride bikes, and drive cars that can create tensions leading to violence. There will always be ways to mark status and group affiliation, so that source of conflict will always be present. . . .

When you read the paragraph, you should have determined that the topic sentence is something like this: "The arguments in favor of uniforms are not strong."

The Supporting Details

Your supporting details must be **adequate,** which means you must have enough of them to prove or explain the thesis and each topic sentence to your reader's satisfaction. To appreciate the importance of adequate detail, read the following body paragraph, which does *not* have adequate detail.

> Proponents of school uniforms say that uniforms reduce gang influence, that they minimize violence by reducing some of the sources of conflict among students, and that they help identify those who are trespassing on school property. It is true that gang affiliation can be signaled by clothing and that students have been attacked because of what they wear. However, uniforms will not necessarily address this problem. There will always be ways to mark status and group affiliation, so that source of conflict will always be present. As for trespassers, much of the serious violence in schools is begun by the students themselves, not by trespassers.

Notice how much more convincing the following paragraph is because of the more substantial supporting details.

> Proponents of school uniforms say that uniforms reduce gang influence, that they minimize violence by reducing some of the sources of conflict among students, and that they help identify those who are trespassing on school property. It is true that gang affiliation can be signaled by clothing and that students have been attacked because of what they wear. However, uniforms will not necessarily address this problem because students are still free to wear jewelry, watches, shoes, and coats for which they can be the targets of violence. They can also carry backpacks, ride bikes, and drive cars that can create tensions leading to violence. There will always be ways to mark status and group affiliation, so that source of conflict will always be present. As for trespassers, school officials, teachers, and security guards know who does and does not belong on school grounds, and if they do not, then identification cards can be issued to address the problem. Further, much of the serious violence in schools is begun by the students themselves, not by trespassers.

Writers have many strategies for providing adequate detail, including describing, telling a story, giving examples, explaining causes and/or effects, showing similarities and/or differences, and showing how something is made or done.

Chapter 6 tells more about strategies for providing adequate supporting details.

In addition to being adequate, supporting details must be **relevant,** which means they must be directly related to both the thesis and the topic sentence of the paragraph they appear in. For example, a paragraph with the topic sentence, "Perhaps more important is the fact that a school-uniform policy takes away choice" should not include detail about whether or not uniforms improve grades. This detail is not relevant to the topic sentence, and including it will sidetrack your reader.

Finally, body paragraphs and supporting details should be presented in a logical order, perhaps one of the following:

- In order of importance (from the least significant to the most significant point)—An essay arguing against restricting immigration might begin with the least compelling reasons and move on to the most compelling reasons.

- In time order (from the first event to the last event)—A story can begin with the first event and proceed in sequence to the last event.

- From general to specific (from a general statement to specific examples) or from specific to general (from specific examples to general statements)—An essay explaining the value of a liberal arts education can first state that a liberal arts education makes a person versatile, and then give specific examples of that versatility. Or it can first give examples of the benefits of a liberal arts education and then conclude with the statement that the education makes a person versatile.

- In order across space (from near to far, front to back, left to right, and so forth)—A real estate brochure describing a house can arrange details from room to room.

- In a problem–solution order (a statement of a problem followed by an explanation of a solution)—A magazine article about Americans' lack of physical fitness might first explain the problem and then offer suggestions for solving it.

- In a cause-and-effect order (an explanation of why an event occurs followed by an explanation of the results of that event)—A research paper about the Nixon presidency could give the causes of the Watergate scandal and go on to note the effects of the scandal on American politics.

The Conclusion

MYTH: After making their last point, writers should just stop.

The end of an essay is the **conclusion.** Conclusions are important because final impressions are important. To realize this, think back to the last movie or television show you watched that ended badly. Remember how let down you felt?

You do not want to leave your reader feeling let down because a negative final impression can undermine the effectiveness of the entire essay. Instead, provide closure, a sense of comfortable completeness—like that provided in this conclusion from "The Uniform Solution," an essay that appears next.

> The problems in our schools mirror problems in the larger society, and these problems must be addressed. Courses in conflict resolution, programs to help students elevate their self-esteem, additional extracurricular activities, and secure schools will go a long way to solving the problems. School uniforms, however, are likely to create more problems than they solve.

Chapter 7 explains strategies for writing conclusions.

 **A SAMPLE ESSAY**

The sample paragraphs in the preceding sections were taken from the essay that follows. (The thesis and topic sentences are underlined as a study aid.)

> ### The Uniform Solution
>
> *Rachel Billey*
>
> Material to stimulate interest.
>
> [1]Right now, something is terribly wrong in our public schools: test scores are down, attendance is dropping, violence is increasing, students are bored and angst-ridden, teachers are demoralized, and parents are frustrated, angry, and worried. Because the problems are multifaceted, the solutions are likely to be complex. However, many are still looking to the quick fix, in this case wearing school uniforms. Uniforms have long been worn by students in private schools, but lately more people are calling for them in public schools. Advocates claim that uniforms will solve everything from low self-esteem and poor grades to minor discipline problems and outbursts of serious violence. When pressed to back up their claims, however, the advocates can do little more than cite anecdotal evidence, because there is no proof that uniforms accomplish all that some say they do. <u>In fact, requiring public school students to wear uniforms will create a new set of problems.</u>
>
> [2]Unlike private schools, public schools cannot require students to wear uniforms. Certainly, public schools can establish and enforce

reasonable dress codes, but because the Constitution guarantees everyone's right to a public education, those who object to wearing uniforms for religious or other compelling reasons cannot be kept out of school. This means that public schools can do little more than *urge* students to wear uniforms. If many choose not to, what is accomplished? If some students wear uniforms and others do not, the chances are good that the two groups of students will be treated differently by teachers and administrators. They will likely give preferential treatment to those who wear the recommended uniforms. After all, these are the students that teachers and administrators favor, the ones who do as they are told. Those who choose not to wear uniforms can easily become second-class citizens because they will be perceived as the trouble-makers, as the ones who do not follow the rules. Thus, uniforms in public schools are likely to create a two-tiered caste system and promote preferential treatment.

> The supporting details are developed with a cause-and-effect strategy.

³Perhaps more important is the fact that a school-uniform policy eliminates opportunity for self-expression. The elimination of self-expression is worrisome because school already demands so much conformity: everyone takes the same classes, keeps the same hours, chooses from the same activities, behaves according to the same rules, and learns the same material. School should help young people express their individuality and creativity so they become comfortable with their personal styles and learn to appreciate the differences around them, but how can they do that if everything about the institution calls for conformity? Allowing students to choose what to wear affords them a harmless respite from the conformity inherent in so much of public education.

> The supporting details explain why eliminating self-expression is a problem.

⁴Proponents of school uniforms say that uniforms reduce gang influence, that they minimize violence by reducing some of the sources of conflict among students, and that they help identify those who are trespassing on school property. It is true that gang affiliation can be signaled by clothing and that students have been attacked because of what they wear. However, uniforms will not necessarily address this problem because students are still free to wear jewelry, watches, shoes, and coats for which they can be the targets of violence. They can also carry backpacks, ride bikes, and drive cars that can create tensions leading to violence. There will always be ways to mark status and group affiliation, so that source of conflict will always be present. As for trespassers, school officials, teachers, and security guards know who does and does not belong on school grounds, and if they do not, then identification cards can be issued to address the problem. Further, much of the serious violence in schools is begun by the students themselves, not by trespassers.

> The topic sentence is implied. The supporting details mention and refute opposing arguments.

The supporting details are arranged in a cause-and-effect pattern.

⁵<u>Another argument cited in favor of uniforms is the reduced cost of buying school clothes, once the need to purchase the latest fashion is eliminated. This benefit is probably real, but it does not offset the drawbacks of uniforms, particularly students' loss of the freedom to express themselves and the ability to exert their independence in harmless ways.</u> After all, students express their personalities and independence in the way they dress. Deprive them of that means of expression, and they will find another, perhaps more dramatic way to exert their independence, including tattoos, body piercing, and drug use. Yes, some of that does go on today even without uniforms, but the practices are likely to increase if students are denied a less harmful means of self-expression.

The supporting details explain why eliminating stress associated with clothing is not desirable.

⁶<u>Proponents of uniforms are also fond of noting that they take a great deal of pressure off of students because they eliminate the stress associated with dressing to keep up with others. This is probably true. However, it may not be desirable to eliminate this form of stress.</u> Sure, while they are in school, students can avoid the stress of "competitive dressing." However, once out of school, they may actually be at a disadvantage because they never learned how to deal with this aspect of a competitive social environment and how to be at peace with themselves, regardless of their manner of dress. In college and in the workplace, they will be confronted with the very stress they could avoid in high school. Only now the stakes are higher and the coping strategies are not in place. In short, how will students learn if school officials force everyone to look alike?

The conclusion provides closure by suggesting alternatives and restating the thesis.

⁷The problems in our schools mirror problems in the larger society, and these problems must be addressed. Courses in conflict resolution, programs to help students elevate their self-esteem, additional extracurricular activities, and secure schools will go a long way to solving the problems. School uniforms are likely to create more problems than they solve.

TEST YOURSELF: Identify Essay Parts

As you have just read, essays often have an introduction, body paragraphs, and conclusion. Look at three editorials in your local newspaper and answer the following questions about each one:

1. Is there a separate introduction? If so, which paragraph(s) form the introduction? What do you think of that introduction? Why?

2. If there is no separate introduction, should there be? Why or why not?

3. Do the body paragraphs do a good job of proving the writer's points? Explain.

4. Is there a separate conclusion? If so, does it create a strong final impression? Explain.

5. If there is no separate conclusion, should there be? Explain.

Part I

A Troubleshooting Guide to Prewriting

Has this happened to you? You write some sentences, but when you read the material over, you hate it. You wad up the paper or hit the delete key, and then you begin again. But the same process repeats itself—over and over. This is writer's block. Or perhaps you never get anything on paper or on the computer screen. Instead, you just stare at the blank page or screen, trying to squeeze out ideas. This, too, is writer's block. Fortunately, you can banish writer's block with the strategies described in this section on prewriting. (**Prewriting** refers to the ways writers discover ideas to write about.)

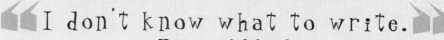 I don't know what to write.

Have you tried these?

- Freewriting **(p. 23)**
- Clustering **(p. 24)**
- Brainstorming **(p. 27)**
- Talking to Other People **(p. 29)**

How do I write a thesis?

Have you tried these?

- Noting Your Main Points **(p. 36)**
- Limiting Your Topic **(p. 36)**
- Using Specific Words **(p. 36)**
- Considering Your Thesis Tentative **(p. 37)**

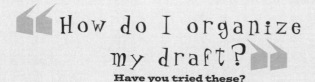 How do I organize my draft?

Have you tried these?

- Checking Your Thesis **(p. 38)**
- Using an Outline Tree **(p. 39)**
- Constructing an Outline Map **(p. 42)**
- Writing an Abstract **(p. 42)**

CHAPTER ONE

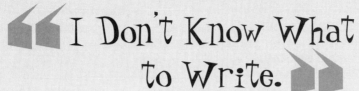

❝I Don't Know What to Write.❞

he terror of the blank page! No, it's not a movie coming soon to a theater near you. It's the fear writers experience when they sit down to write and cannot think of anything to say. Sure, sometimes writers are zapped by the lightning bolt of inspiration, and idea after idea comes tumbling forth. However, inspiration is fickle and cannot be counted on to show up just because you have an essay due a week from Friday. Therefore, if inspiration fails you, take steps to develop ideas on your own. The following strategies, known as **idea generation techniques,** can help you come up with ideas when inspiration does not arrive on time.

FREEWRITE

The act of writing stimulates thought, so when you cannot think of anything to write, start writing anyway. Eventually, ideas will surface. With **freewriting** you write to discover ideas to write about. It works like this: Sit in a quiet spot and write nonstop for about 10 minutes. Record every idea that occurs to you, no matter how silly or irrelevant it seems. Do not stop for any reason. If you run out of ideas, write the days of the week, names of your family members, even "I don't know what to write." Write *anything.* Soon new thoughts will strike you, and you can write about them.

The important thing about freewriting is to be *free,* so make wild statements, write silly notions, or make random associations. Do not evaluate anything; if it occurs to you, write it down. Do not worry about grammar, spelling, punctuation, or neatness—just write ideas the best way you can without worrying over anything.

Here is a freewriting produced to discover ideas for an essay about the effects of computers:

> Computers are wonderful and scarry at the same time. They are great because they make things easier and faster, like writing things and getting info. Lets see, what else? They store info and trade it with other computers so our privacy can be invaded, that's pretty scarry. Lap top computers are big now, you see people use them everywhere. That's good and bad because you can work when its convenient but you also work when you should be resting. This whole Internet thing is wierd. People spend whole days on it. Is that productive or lost time? What else? 1 2 3 4 5 6 7 8 Pornography is a problem on the Internet and kids can get involved. Yuk. Now what else? I'm stuck, I'm stuck. If you don't understand computers, you will have trouble in the job market. I guess that means schools better do a good job of teaching this stuff. Now what? Anything else? Expensive. Who can afford all this computer equipment? Is it just for the rich? I read an articel that said computers are changing the way we communicate. I don't remember what all it said, I should look it up.

Notice that the freewriting unearthed a number of ideas for an essay about the effects of computers: convenience, possible invasion of privacy, changes in the way people work, the time spent on the Internet, changes in the way people communicate, the need for schools to educate children in computer skills, whether or not computer access is just for the rich. These are too many points for one standard college essay, so the writer would choose one or two of them to write about.

Use Looping

With **looping,** you explore a topic in more depth by doing a second and sometimes third freewriting. For example, the previous freewriting on the effects of computers yielded several ideas for writing, including "the time spent on the Internet." To use looping, you would freewrite on this topic for 10 minutes. That second "loop" may yield enough material, or you may freewrite a third loop on an idea that emerged in the second loop. Taken together, all the freewriting loops can bring forth considerable material.

Try Clustering

Clustering lets you see at a glance how ideas relate to one another. To cluster, write in the middle of a page a subject area you want to think about. Then draw a circle around the subject, so you have something that looks like this:

Next, as you think of ideas, connect them to the central circle.

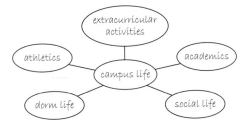

As more ideas occur to you, connect them to the appropriate circles.

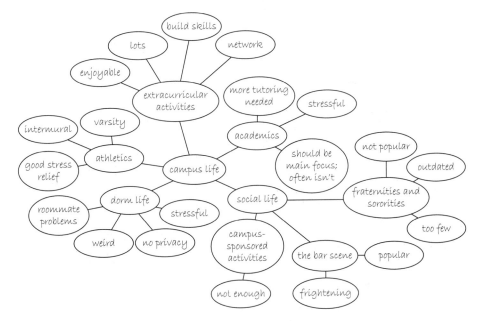

Continue writing ideas and joining them to circles until you can think of nothing else. Then, study your clustering to see if one particular circle with its connecting circles gives you enough to begin a draft. For example, this portion of the previous clustering might serve as a departure point for a draft about the benefits of extracurricular activities.

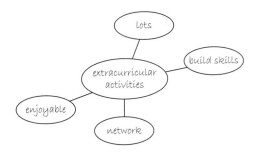

If this clustering does not yield enough ideas for a draft, cluster again to expand the branches:

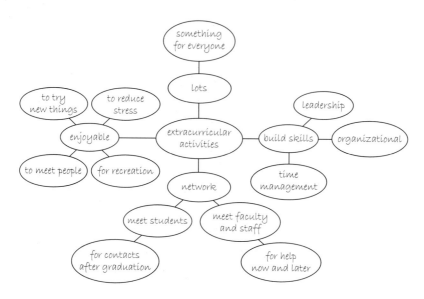

✳ WRITE A LIST

List ideas that occur to you in phrases rather than sentences. Do not censor yourself; write everything you think of. Even if you are sure an idea is terrible, write it anyway because it may prompt you to think of another, more useful idea. Here is an idea generation list for an essay about the effects of being cut from the basketball team:

felt rejected
was embarrassed
disappointed my father
got teased
felt inadequate
gave up basketball forever
decided to go out for cross-country
lost my best friend, who was busy with the team

Next, review your list and cross out ideas you do not want to use and add new ideas that occur to you. If you number the ideas in the list in the order you want to treat them in your draft, you have a scratch outline.

Sometimes you may want to write a second list focusing on only one of the points in your first list. For example, a second list focusing on "lost my best friend, who was busy with the team" could look like this:

Cal had no time for me
practiced every day
couldn't go out at night because of curfew
socialized with his teammates
wouldn't play sports with me because of fear of injuries

BRAINSTORM

To **brainstorm** for ideas, ask yourself questions about your topic. The answers can provide details for your essay. Sometimes the question that offers up the most is the simple question "Why?" In addition, you may find the following questions helpful:

Why did it happen?	What is it similar to?
How did it happen?	What is it different from?
Who was involved?	What are its physical characteristics?
When did it happen?	Why is it important?
Where did it happen?	Who would care about it?
Could it happen again?	What causes it?
What does it mean?	What are its effects?
How does it work?	What is it related to?
Why does this matter to me?	What examples are there?
Why does this matter to my reader?	How can it be explained?
Why is it true?	What controversies are associated with it?

EXAMINE YOUR TOPIC FROM DIFFERENT ANGLES

If you have a broad subject area you want to write about, but you are not sure how to limit the subject, try viewing it from different angles. Asking yourself the following questions can show you how to approach your topic from different perspectives:

1. **How can I describe my subject?** What does it look, smell, taste, sound, and feel like? What are its parts, its color, its size, its shape, and so on?

2. **How can I compare and contrast my subject?** What is it like, and what is it different from? Are the similarities and differences important?

3. **What do I associate my subject with?** What does it make people think of? What is it related to? What does it develop from or lead to?

4. **How can I analyze my subject?** How is it broken down? How does it work? What is it made of? Why is it important?

5. **How can I apply my subject?** What is it good for? Who would find it useful? When is it useful? Does it have social, economic, or political value?

6. **What arguments accompany my subject?** What are the reasons for it? What are the reasons against it? Who is for it? Who is against it? Is it right or wrong? Good or bad? How does it affect society?

After answering these questions, you may have an approach to your subject. Then you can do some additional idea generation for ideas to suit your approach.

✳ Use Questionnaires

Learning what other people think can expose you to fresh perspectives and stimulate your own thinking. To discover what others think, develop a questionnaire for people to complete. This is not a scientific instrument; it is just something to prime your own idea pump. For example, say you want to write about the movie rating system. You could develop the following questionnaire for some students, faculty, family, and friends.

1. What do you think of the current movie rating system that uses the designations G, PG, PG-13, R, and NC-17?
2. Why do you think the way you do?
3. What could be done to improve the system?
4. What aspects of the current system should remain the same? Why?

Your questionnaire should not include too many questions, or people will not bother with it. Nor should you use the answers *instead* of your own thinking; the answers are meant to stimulate your own thinking. Finally, question at least 5 people, so you get a useful number of responses.

✳ Write an Exploratory Draft

When you do not know what to write, sometimes the solution is to get in there and write anyway. You may be one of those people who don't know what they want to say until they say it. If so, sit down and force yourself to write on your topic for about an hour without worrying about how good the material is. The result will be an exploratory draft, a few pages of material reflecting what you currently know. An exploratory draft may yield a thought or two that you can pursue with one of the idea generation techniques in this chapter, or it may yield enough for you to try an outline or rough draft. Remember that your goal is not to produce a first draft of your essay; it is to discover one or more ideas to serve as a departure point.

✳ Relate the Topic to Your Own Experience

Relate the topic to your own experiences so you can write about what you know. For example, if you have been asked to write about modern technology, remember all the trouble your cell phone caused you, and write an essay about how these devices can be more trouble than they are worth. If you have been asked to write about the American educational system, think about your child-care hassles and argue that your college should have a day-care center. A topic that seems formidable at first can be made manageable if it is viewed in the context of your own life experiences.

Talk into a Tape Recorder

Forget writing for a while and try talking. Have a conversation with yourself about your topic by speaking all your thoughts into a tape recorder. Do not censor yourself; just talk about whatever occurs to you, and feel free to be silly, offbeat, funny, dramatic, or outlandish. When you run out of ideas, play back the tape. When you hear a good idea, pause the tape and write the idea down.

Talk to Other People

Discuss your writing topic with friends and relatives. They may be able to suggest ideas. Or have other people ask you the brainstorming questions on page 27.

Write a Poem

Sometimes changing formats can help, so instead of trying to write an essay, write a poem about your topic. Then study it for ideas you can shape and develop in essay form.

Write about Your Block

When all else fails, write about why you can't write. Explain how you feel, what is keeping you from getting ideas, and what you would write if you could. This sheer act of writing can catapult you beyond the block to productive idea generation.

Put Your Writing on the Back Burner

If you do not know what to write, you may need to give your ideas an incubation period. Try going about your normal routine with your writing topic on the back burner. Think about your topic from time to time throughout the day. Many writers get their best ideas while walking the dog, washing the car, sitting in a traffic jam, or cleaning the house. If you feel anxious, exercise to relieve the tension. Of course, if an idea strikes while you are in the middle of something, stop and write the idea down so you do not forget it.

IDENTIFY YOUR PURPOSE AND AUDIENCE

You may have trouble thinking of ideas if you have not clarified your purpose and audience. (see pages 6–9). Responding to the following can help.

1. **To identify your purpose:**
   a. What feelings, ideas, or experiences can I relate to my reader?
   b. Of what can I inform my reader?
   c. Of what can I persuade my reader?
   d. In what way can I entertain my reader?

2. **To identify your audience:**
   a. Who could learn something from my writing?
   b. Who would enjoy reading about my topic?
   c. Who could be influenced to think or act a certain way?
   d. Who is interested in my topic or would find it important?
   e. Who needs to hear what I have to say?

KEEP A JOURNAL

Buy a full-size spiral notebook for keeping a journal or set up a computer file. Write in your journal every day. A journal is not a diary because it is not a record of your daily activities. Instead, it is an account of your thoughts and reactions to events. For example, if you feel compassion for a blind person you saw, describe your feelings. If you are anxious about an upcoming event, explain why you are concerned. If you were recently reminded of a childhood event, describe this memory.

A journal is also a good place to think things through in writing. Is something troubling you? Do you have a problem? Explore the issues in your journal, and you may achieve new insights. In addition, if you are working on a writing project, a journal is an ideal place to try out an approach to part of the draft, or tinker with a revision. A journal is also an excellent place to respond to what goes on in your classes: Summarize class notes, respond to reading assignments, and react to lectures. Journal activities like these will help you learn course material.

Because your journal is meant for you and not for a reader, you do not need to revise and edit anything. Just write your ideas down any way that suits you because you are your primary audience this time. Later, if you are looking for a writing topic, review your journal for ideas.

Set aside at least 15 minutes every day to write in your journal. If you have trouble thinking of what to write, try one of the following suggestions:

1. Write about something that angers you, that pleases you, or that frustrates you.

2. Describe the ideal college education.

3. Write about some change you would like to make in yourself.

4. Look at a newspaper and respond to a headline.

5. Write about someone you admire.

6. Describe your life as you would like it to be in five years.

7. Tell about one thing the world could do without.

8. Record a vivid childhood memory.

9. Describe the best and worst features of your school.

10. Describe your current writing process, including what you do to generate ideas, draft, revise, and edit.

11. Describe one piece of legislation you wish you could draft. Explain how it would improve the world.

12. Record your reactions to your writing class so far: What do you find confusing? What has been helpful? What topics would you like to cover? What do you think of the pace of instruction?

Combine Techniques

Combine techniques any way you like. Perhaps you will begin with freewriting and then brainstorm. Or maybe you will talk into a tape recorder and then list. Experiment until you find the combination of techniques that works the best.

Develop Your Own Writing Topic

If you must come up with your own writing topic, some of the following strategies may help.

1. Try freewriting (see page 23). Begin something like this: "I need a writing topic. Let's see, maybe I could write about. . . . "

2. Try clustering (page 24). Begin by placing one of these subjects in a circle in the center of the page: education, athletics, friendship, television, movies, family, automobiles, teenagers, memories, technology, the environment.

3. Skim magazines and newspapers for ideas. An article on the Olympics could prompt you to write that the government should subsidize athletes.

4. Consult your journal for topic ideas (see page 30).

5. Fill in the blanks in the following sentences.

a. I'll never forget the time I _____.

b. The best thing about _____ is _____.

c. The worst thing about _____ is _____.

d. My most embarrassing (or proudest) moment occurred when _____
_____.

e. I wish I could change _____.

f. After _____ I changed my mind about _____.

g. _____ is the most unforgettable person I know.

h. _____ is the most _____ I know.

i. The best way to _____ is _____.

j. Few people understand the true meaning of _____.

k. What this country needs is _____.

l. Without _____, life would be very different.

m. _____ made a lasting impression on me.

n. Few people understand the differences between _____ and
_____.

o. _____ and _____ are more alike than people realize.

Filling in the blanks in these sentences will not give you ready-to-use topics, but the completed sentences will *suggest* topics. For example, consider this completed sentence:

I wish I could change the way public education is funded in this state.

This sentence could lead to the following topic:

Rather than using the property tax, this state should finance public education with an increased income tax.

6. Make a list of questions or problems, and use one of the questions or problems as a departure point for additional idea generation. For example, your list could include some of the following:

a. Do nice people really finish last?

b. What is the best way to find a job?

c. Why do women wear makeup when men don't?

d. How can I improve my conversation skills?

e. Is it too late to save our environment?

f. Why do so few people vote?

g. Why are violent movies so popular?

TROUBLESHOOTING WITH A COMPUTER

If you use a computer, you may like the following strategies.

FREEWRITE

With a blank screen, write whatever comes to mind about your subject (or even your lack of a subject). Do not go back with the delete key, the backspace key, or the left arrow key. Just write for about ten minutes. Then get a printout, and read what you have typed. Underline usable ideas. Perhaps there will be enough to get you started. If not, do a second freewriting focusing on the underlined ideas. (For more on freewriting, see page 23.)

WRITE BLINDFOLDED

No, you don't really blindfold yourself or even close your eyes. Just find the switch that controls the brightness of the monitor and turn it all the way down until the screen is dark. Then type for ten minutes, just as you would if you were freewriting. When you are done, your screen may look like this:

I kdon;t know what to write I think I;ll write about the problems of students are getting wripped off on the fees and tuition being changerd.

That's not a problem. You can still detect the seeds of good ideas to expand on in a draft or in a second blindfolded writing.

WRITE E-MAIL

Write an e-mail to a friend or classmate and discuss your writing topic. Mention the ideas you currently have and ask for a response to those ideas and for some additional ideas to consider.

LIST AND WRITE A SCRATCH OUTLINE

You may appreciate listing on the computer because ideas can be easily reorganized and deleted to get a neat, sequenced list of ideas. Just write the first idea that comes to mind. A word or a phrase will do just fine. Press the enter or return key. Write another idea, and press the enter or return key. Repeat these steps until you run out of ideas. Use your delete key(s) to eliminate ideas you want to strike from your list. Next, study your list and decide what order is suggested. Try out the order using the copy-move sequence. Rearrange your list as often as you like until you have a suitable scratch outline to guide your first draft.

USE THE INTERNET

The Internet can be a helpful resource for writers who need ideas. In particular, you might try the following:

- *Surf the Internet.* Type a subject into a search engine and scan the titles returned for possible writing topics or ideas for developing a topic. Four popular search engines are

  Alta Vista: <www.altavista.com>
  Google: <www.google.com>
  Yahoo: <www.yahoo.com>
  All the Web: <www.alltheweb.com>

- *Browse news sites.* Scan one of these popular news sites for information on current events, health, business, and entertainment. You might get several writing ideas.

  Yahoo news: <news.yahoo.com/?u>
  Reuters News Service: <www.reuters.com/news.jhtml>
  Google News: <news.google.com>

- *Browse electronic newspapers and magazines.* Try one of these sites:

  For newspapers around the country and world:
  <www.refdesk.com/paper.html>
  An online magazine:
  slate: <www.slate.msn.com>
  A national newspaper: <usatoday.com>

- *Browse websites with links to varied content.* These two sites, in particular, may give you writing ideas:

  Science and Technology Daily: <scitechdaily.com>
  Arts and Letters Daily: <aldaily.com>

CHAPTER TWO

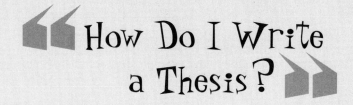

"How Do I Write a Thesis?"

You might know in your own mind what your essay is about, but that is not enough. You need to convey that idea to your reader in a clear, appealing way—and that's where your **thesis** comes in. Your thesis is the statement of your essay's focus (see page 11), and it frequently appears in your opening paragraph—the **introduction** (see page 10). Because your thesis guides the course of your essay, it must be crafted with care. The suggestions in this chapter can help.

STUDY YOUR IDEA GENERATION MATERIAL

You may be tempted to base your thesis on the point you generated the most ideas for, but that point may not be your best choice. Perhaps you have too much material for the length you are working with, or perhaps that point holds little interest for your reader. Study your idea generation material carefully with your reader in mind before deciding on your thesis idea.

WRITE A TWO-PART THESIS

One part of your thesis should give the topic you are discussing, and the other part should note your assertion about that topic. In the following examples, the topic is underlined once, and the assertion is underlined twice.

The television ratings system does not serve the purpose it was intended to serve.

The federal government should outlaw Internet gambling.

Although textbooks cost a great deal of money, they are one of the best bargains in education.

Teachers should not get preferential parking on this campus.

Note the Main Points That Will Be Made in Your Essay

In addition to noting your topic and your assertion about that topic, your thesis can indicate the main points you will cover in your body paragraphs (although it does not have to do this). In the following example, the designated main points are underlined.

> Year-round schools are a good idea because <u>children would not forget material over long summer breaks</u>, <u>child care would not be a problem for working parents</u>, and <u>a greater number of elective courses could be offered.</u>

Limit Your Topic to Something Manageable

Avoid treating more than one topic or more than one assertion. Also avoid single topics that are too broad. Treating more than one topic, more than one assertion, or a very broad topic requires you to write too much, or it forces you into a very general, superficial treatment of your topic.

More than one topic: To revitalize the city, tax incentives should be offered to new businesses, and more parking should be offered downtown.

Better (one topic): To revitalize the city, tax incentives should be offered to new businesses.

Better (one topic): To revitalize the city, more parking should be offered downtown.

More than one assertion: Voters would be less apathetic if campaign finance laws were changed, and if candidates debated more often.

Better (one assertion): Voters would be less apathetic if campaign finance laws were changed.

Better (one assertion): Voters would be less apathetic if candidates debated more often.

Too broad: The American political system needs to be overhauled.

Better: The electoral college is no longer a sensible way to elect a president.

Express your Assertion in Specific Words

Words like *good, nice, awesome, bad,* and *interesting* are too vague to give your reader a clear indication of your assertion, so opt instead for more specific words and phrases.

Vague Jennifer Juarez makes a <u>good</u> candidate for City Council.

Better Jennifer Juarez is a qualified candidate for City Council because of her extensive political background.

Vague New York's Metropolitan Museum is an <u>awesome</u> place.

Better Because of the number and variety of its holdings, New York's Metropolitan Museum is a national treasure.

Avoid Factual Statements

If your thesis is a statement of indisputable fact, your essay will have nowhere to go.

Factual statement: The zoning board must decide whether to approve a housing development on Route 193.

Better: The zoning board should approve the housing development on Route 193.

Avoid Announcing Your Intentions

Thesis statements that include wordings like "This essay will show," "In the following paragraphs I will explain," and "My purpose is to demonstrate" are best reserved for scientific and technical papers.

Announcement: The purpose of this paper is to show why state lotteries are harmful to the average person.

Better: State lotteries are harmful to the average person.

Consider Your Thesis to Be Tentative

During drafting and revising, everything is part of a process of discovery and, therefore, subject to change. Your thesis, no matter how carefully you crafted it, is tentative. It may change later, as new insights occur to you.

TROUBLESHOOTING WITH A COMPUTER

If you compose at the computer, try the following strategies.

E-Mail a Friend or Classmate

If you have trouble composing a thesis, e-mail your idea generation material to a friend or classmate. Ask that person to review the material and identify one or more thesis statements that seem to emerge from that material.

Use the Internet

For additional information on how to write a thesis, visit these websites:

- Capital Community College's Guide to Grammar and Writing— <www.ccc.commnet.edu/grammar>. Click on "index" and then "thesis."
- Purdue University's Online Writing Lab—<owl.english.purdue.edu>. In the "search" box, type "thesis."

Chapter Three

"How Do I Get My Ideas to Fit Together?" »

O kay, so you've come up with good ideas and now you need to get your ideas to hang together in a coherent whole. The strategies in this chapter can help.

Check Your Thesis

Your thesis tells what your essay is about. (For more on the thesis, see Chapter 2.) If your ideas do not come together, the problem may be with your thesis. Check your thesis against the guidelines that follow and make any necessary revisions.

1. **Be sure you <u>have</u> a thesis.** Can you point to or write out a specific sentence or two that expresses the focus of your writing? If not, your ideas may be nothing more than a collection of loosely related thoughts that seem confused because they do not develop one central focus.

2. **Be sure your thesis expresses an idea worthy of discussion,** something that is disputed or something in need of explanation. For more on this point, see page 11.

3. **Be sure your thesis does not take in too much territory,** or you will be forced to bring in too many ideas, which can create disorder.

Thesis covering too much territory: High school was a traumatic experience.

Acceptable thesis: My first high school track meet was a traumatic experience.

The first thesis requires the writer to cover events spanning four years— a great deal for one essay. The second thesis sets up a more reasonable goal— covering the events of one afternoon.

38

WRITE A SCRATCH OUTLINE

To write a scratch outline, list all your most important points. Then review the list and number the points in the order you will handle them in your writing. A scratch outline can be made quickly, and many writers find it useful. However, because the outline is not very detailed (it covers only the main points), other writers find it does not provide enough structure. If you are one of the latter, you may prefer one of the other outlining techniques described in this chapter.

CONSTRUCT AN OUTLINE TREE

The outline tree provides a visual representation of how ideas relate to each other. To construct a tree, write your thesis on the page:

A refundable deposit should be added to the price of products in glass containers.

Next, branch your main ideas off from your thesis idea:

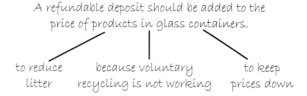

Then, branch supporting ideas off from your main ideas:

The outline tree shows you how ideas relate to each other so that when drafting, you avoid skipping randomly from one idea to another.

✳ COMPLETE AN OUTLINE WORKSHEET

With an outline worksheet, you can plan your draft in a fair amount of detail without the roman numerals, letters, and numbers of a formal outline. To use the worksheet, copy the form in Figure 1 on p. 41 and fill in the blanks with words and phrases that indicate the points you will make in the draft. Then write the draft using the worksheet as a guide.

✳ WRITE AN INFORMAL OUTLINE

Writers who are uncomfortable with the formal outline that uses roman numerals, capital and lower case letters, and numbers often like the informal outline that lists and groups the most important ideas. Typically, an informal outline includes

- The thesis idea
- The major points to support the thesis
- Some of the ideas that support the major points

Here is an example of an informal outline for the essay on page 16.

Thesis idea

Public school students should not have to wear uniforms.

Introduction

Mention the problems public schools face (attendance, violence, low test scores, demoralized teachers and students) and explain that uniforms are not the solution to these problems.

Body paragraphs

The Constitution does not allow public school students to be forced to wear uniforms.
—Some students will wear and some won't.
—Preferential treatment will result.
If everyone dresses the same, there will be no self-expression.
—Students need to express their individuality in a harmless way.
—Most other aspects of education require conformity.
Deal with argument that uniforms save money and eliminate "clothing competition."
—The savings isn't worth the problems uniforms cause.
—People need to learn how to handle competition.

Conclusion

The problems in our schools must be solved but uniforms won't do it.

FIGURE 1 *Outline Worksheet*

Paragraph I

   1. Opening comments to stimulate reader's interest:————————.

   ———————————————————————————————

   ———————————————————————————————

   2. Thesis statement:————————————————————————.

   ———————————————————————————————

   ———————————————————————————————

Paragraph II

   1. Main point (topic sentence idea): ————————————————.

   ———————————————————————————————

   ———————————————————————————————

   2. Supporitng details to develop main point:————————————.

   ———————————————————————————————

   ———————————————————————————————

Paragraph III

   1. Main point (topic sentence idea):—————————————————.

   ———————————————————————————————

   ———————————————————————————————

   2. Supporitng details to develop main point:—————————————.

   ———————————————————————————————

   ———————————————————————————————

   ———————————————————————————————

Note: Continue in this way until all main points are treated.

Final paragraph

Ideas to bring writing to closure:————————————————————.

———————————————————————————————

———————————————————————————————

———————————————————————————————

CONSTRUCT AN OUTLINE MAP

To develop the map, use your list of generated ideas to fill in a copy of the form shown in Figure 2 on page 43.

To complete the map, write in your thesis and place one main point at the top of each column. (If you have two main points, you will have two columns; three main points will mean three columns, and so on.) In the columns under each main point, write the supporting ideas that will develop the main point. Then note what your concluding point(s) will be.

The beauty of the outline map is that before you begin drafting you can check the relevance of ideas by checking what is in each column against the main point at the top, and you can check the relevance of each main point by comparing it to the thesis.

You can write your draft from the map by allowing each column to be a body paragraph, with each main point expressed in a topic sentence.

WRITE AN ABSTRACT

An **abstract** is a very brief summary. Before you draft, write a one-paragraph abstract of what you plan to say in your writing. Include only the main points, and leave out the details that will expand on those points. Then read over your abstract to check that the main points follow logically one to the next. If they do not, try another abstract, placing your ideas in a different order. When you draft, you can flesh out the abstract into a full-length piece of writing.

TROUBLESHOOTING WITH A COMPUTER

Computers can be very handy for helping writers organize their ideas.

THE SCRATCH OUTLINE

If you use a computer to generate ideas by listing, you can turn your list into a scratch outline very easily. Use the delete key to eliminate the ideas that you do not want to use (and if new ideas occur to you, add them to the list). Then using the copy-paste command, arrange the ideas in the order you want to treat them in your writing.

THE OUTLINE PROGRAM

If your computer has an outline program, use it to fill in the various levels designated by roman numerals, letters, and numbers. Study the results and expand and delete sublevels as necessary.

FIGURE 2 *Outline Map*

Thesis: _____

Main Point (Topic Sentence Idea)	Main Point (Topic Sentence Idea)	Main Point (Topic Sentence Idea)	Main Point (Topic Sentence Idea)
Supporting Detail	Supporting Detail	Supporting Detail	Supporting Detail

Concluding points: _____

_____

_____

_____

CREATE YOUR OWN OUTLINE FILE

If your word processing program does not include an outline feature, develop your own outline form, using roman numerals, letters, and numbers. Save the form as a file you can retrieve whenever you want to outline. You can also create forms and files for the outline map and outline worksheet.

Use the Internet

If you want to learn the mechanics of writing a formal outline, visit Purdue University's Online Writing Lab at <owl.english.purdue.edu/handouts/general/gl_outlin.html>.

Part II

A Troubleshooting Guide to Drafting

Drafting is your first attempt to write your ideas on the page or computer screen. Because it is your *first* effort, your draft will probably have many problems. That's normal. In fact, most people write very rough first drafts and then rework them until they are polished and reader-ready. In other words, do not feel discouraged if your drafting yields a very ragged piece of writing. Rough though it is, that draft is useful raw material that you can refine.

❝ I know what I want to say, but I can't say it. ❞

Have you tried these?

- ❏ Switching tools **(p. 48)**
- ❏ Writing a letter **(p. 48)**
- ❏ Walking away **(p. 49)**
- ❏ Writing fast **(p. 50)**

❝ How do I write an introduction? ❞

Have you tried these?

- ❏ Providing background **(p. 52)**
- ❏ Telling a story **(p. 53)**
- ❏ Using a quotation **(p. 53)**
- ❏ Using statistics **(p. 54)**

❝ I need more details. ❞

Have you tried these?

- ❏ Using your experience **(p. 56)**
- ❏ Observing **(p. 56)**
- ❏ Describing **(p. 57)**
- ❏ Giving examples **(p. 58)**

❝ How do I write a conclusion? ❞

Have you tried these?

- ❏ Providing a summary **(p. 64)**
- ❏ Emphasizing a point **(p. 64)**
- ❏ Asking a question **(p. 65)**
- ❏ Keeping it short **(p. 66)**

❝ I can't think of the right word. ❞

Have you tried these?

- ❏ Using a natural style **(p. 67)**
- ❏ Asking for help **(p. 68)**
- ❏ Freewriting **(p. 68)**
- ❏ Skipping it **(p. 68)**

CHAPTER FOUR

"I Know What I Want to Say, But I Can't Say It."

S O you think you know what you want to say, and you sit down with plenty of fresh writing paper, pencils sharpened to a lethal point, and a bowl of Doritos. Then disaster strikes: You know what you want to say, but the words don't come out right—or they don't come out at all. If this happens to you, know that you are not alone. Plenty of writers experience the same block. To get past the block, use the techniques described in this chapter.

GET RID OF DISTRACTIONS

Are you trying to write with headphones on? With TV on in the background? With your roommate rummaging around looking for a missing left sneaker? With the street department outside tearing up the pavement with an air hammer? Few people can write when distractions disrupt their focus, so getting past writer's block may be as simple as finding a place to write that is free of distractions.

SET INTERMEDIATE GOALS FOR YOURSELF

At the beginning of a writing project, the finish line can seem so far away that we feel stress. This stress can lead to writer's block. Try breaking the task down into manageable steps. For example, the first time you sit down, tell yourself you will just come up with five ideas and a scratch outline. The second time, you will just draft the introduction. The third time, you will draft two more paragraphs. If you work toward the completion of intermediate goals, the project will be less intimidating.

✳ ALLOW YOUR DRAFT TO BE ROUGH

If you find yourself starting a draft, crumpling up the paper and pitching it to the floor, starting another draft, crumpling up the paper and pitching it to the floor, starting another draft and so forth, you may be expecting too much too soon. Remember, a first draft is *supposed* to be rough. Instead of wadding up that draft, force yourself to go from start to finish in one sitting to get raw material to shape during the revision process that comes later.

✳ WRITE IN A NEW PLACE

A change of scene can help a writer break through a block, so if you usually write in one place, try another. Go to the library, the park, or a local diner. If you write in your room, try the lounge or a classroom, or the dining hall. A new locale can give you a fresh perspective.

✳ SWITCH YOUR WRITING TOOLS

If you write with a pen, try a pencil or a computer. If you use a computer, try a pen. If you like lined paper, try unlined. If you like legal pads, try stationery. Do anything to make the writing *feel* different.

✳ WRITE ON A DAILY SCHEDULE

Professional writers are disciplined about their work. They make themselves sit down at the same time each day to write for a specific number of hours. Follow the lead of the professionals and push past the block by forcing yourself to write at a certain time each day for a specific length of time.

✳ WRITE A LETTER TO A FRIEND

Sometimes we think of the reader at the other end judging our work, and we freeze. Try writing your draft as if it were a letter to a friend—a letter to someone who cares about you and who will value you regardless of how well you write. When your audience is shifted to a person you feel comfortable with, you can relax and allow the words to emerge. After writing a draft this way, you can revise to make your work suitable for your intended reader and to shape it into an essay or other appropriate form.

❋WRITE FOR YOURSELF INSTEAD OF FOR A READER

Forget your reader for a while and write the draft in a way that pleases *you*. Be your own audience at first. Later when you polish your work, you can make the changes necessary for the audience you are aiming for.

❋USE A NATURAL STYLE

Sometimes writers try so hard to achieve what they think is a "college" style that the strain causes a block. To solve this problem, write as you normally speak, and the words should flow more easily. After drafting this way, revise if the writing is too conversational or informal.

Unnatural: The garrulous male juvenile who, upon cursory examination gave the appearance of being about 12, nettled the orator.

More natural: The talkative boy, who looked about 12, annoyed the speaker.

❋SPEAK INTO A TAPE RECORDER

Sometimes we have trouble writing, but we do not have trouble talking. Try speaking your draft into a tape recorder. Afterwards, you can transcribe the tape to get your draft.

❋REREAD OFTEN

If you get blocked in the middle, go back and reread your draft from the beginning. Doing so can give you momentum and propel you past the block. Rereading can be a reminder of your thesis, purpose, and organizational strategy, a reminder that keeps you on track.

❋WALK AWAY

When the words won't come, you may need time away to relax and let things simmer. Take a walk, listen to music, play tennis, take a shower, make a sandwich, read a magazine, clean a drawer, or pot a plant. Do anything to clear your mind for a while. Time away can provide an incubation period, so when you start to write again you are no longer stuck.

WRITE THE INTRODUCTION LAST

If you're stuck on the introduction, write the rest of your essay and then go back to it. With the rest of your draft complete, you may find your introduction easier to handle than it was before. (If you write your introduction last, write a thesis on scratch paper so you have a focus for your draft.)

BEGIN IN THE MIDDLE

Begin writing whatever point you feel confident writing and go from there. Starting with an idea you can write—no matter where in the draft it falls—can propel you forward.

CONCENTRATE ON WHAT YOU CAN DO AND SKIP WHAT YOU CAN'T DO

You can start out just fine, but begin to struggle along the way and eventually come to a full stop. Why does a good start fizzle? This may happen because you dwell on the trouble spots and lose momentum. To solve this problem, skip the trouble spots: If you cannot think of the right word, leave a blank and add it later; if you sense some detail is not working, underline it for later consideration and press on; if the right approach to your introduction escapes you, begin with your second paragraph and go on from there. You will make more progress by focusing on what you *can* do and leaving the problems behind to deal with later.

RESIST THE TEMPTATION TO REWRITE AS YOU DRAFT

If you constantly rewrite what you have already written, you can get stuck in one place—maybe polishing the introduction over and over, or perhaps tinkering endlessly with the detail to support your first point. While some writers do well if they revise as they go, others get bogged down. If you get bogged down, try pushing forward even if what you have already written is in pretty sorry shape. You can revise the rough spots later.

WRITE FAST AND DON'T LOOK BACK

If you write fast, you will have no time to worry about how well you are saying things. You will only be able to get things down the best way you can at the moment. Later when you revise, you can rework things as needed.

✳ WRITE AN OUTLINE

If you have generated a number of good ideas and you still have trouble writing a draft, you may be unsure what idea you should write first, second, third, and so on. An outline can help. (For information on outlining, consult Chapter 3.)

✳ RETURN TO IDEA GENERATION

You may *not* have a clear enough idea of what you want to say, so you may need to return to idea generation. Try a favorite technique to clarify your thinking or to flesh out some existing ideas. Or try a technique you have not used before (see Chapter 1 for suggestions).

 TROUBLESHOOTING WITH A COMPUTER

If you like to compose at the computer, the next techniques can be helpful.

SPLIT YOUR SCREEN

On one part of the screen, display your outline or idea generation material; on the other side, display your draft. This way, you can easily refer to your prewriting material as you write. You can also place your thesis in one of the screens to help you stay on track as you draft.

WRITE INVISIBLE NOTES

Many word processing programs allow you to write notes that appear on your screen but not on the printed page. If you want to remember a question, record an idea, or make a comment for later consideration, and you do not want to interrupt your drafting, use this capability to write on your draft. The comments will not appear on your paper copy, but they will be saved for you to come back to.

CUT AND PASTE

If you generate ideas on the computer, you can cut and paste some or all of that material into a first draft. Of course, you will need to revise that material later, but it can work well as a departure point.

USE THE INTERNET

The following site has information on what causes writer's block and how to prevent it and deal with it: <www.suite101.com/welcome.cfm/writers_block>.

CHAPTER FIVE

"I'm Having Trouble with My Introduction."

The first day of school, the first day on a new job, a first date—starting out can be hard. Starting out a piece of writing can also be difficult, even if you have generated plenty of ideas. The strategies in this chapter can help.

EXPLAIN WHY YOUR TOPIC IS IMPORTANT

Why should anyone take time to read your essay? Let your readers know why your topic is important, and you can engage their interest. Say your essay will explain to residents of your town how they can eliminate cigarette advertising on billboards. Your introduction can explain why residents should want to eliminate this advertising in the first place.

> Other than the tobacco companies and a few nicotine addicts who live in denial, few people dispute the fact that cigarettes are a serious—even a deadly—health hazard. Because cigarettes are so dangerous, laws prohibit their advertising on television. Unfortunately, a similar ban does not exist for print media. As a result, many people are enticed to begin smoking after viewing the ads that promise everything from "pure smoking pleasure" to fun, friends, and romance. Teenagers and younger children are particularly vulnerable to the seductive advertising, and we must protect them. While we cannot force national advertisers to stop running magazine advertisements, we can lobby local officials to ban cigarette advertising on billboards in our town.

PROVIDE BACKGROUND INFORMATION

What should your reader know to appreciate or understand your topic? What information would establish a context for your essay? The answers to these questions can provide background information in the introduction. For example, assume you will argue that more federal money should be spent to educate children about the dangers of tobacco. Your introduction could supply background information about past efforts in this area.

> In the late 1990s President Clinton began an initiative to reduce tobacco use by children. The public was invited to comment, public officials made grand speeches, the press covered the proceedings extensively, and the result was a few Food and Drug Administration efforts to reduce access and limit the appeal of tobacco products for children. Basically, all this amounted to was some billboards and public service announcements on television. The effects have been minimal, and the public health crisis is worsening as children start smoking at younger ages. Clearly, the federal government must devote considerably more money and resources to educating children about tobacco.

✳ Tell a Story

Create interest in your topic by telling a story that is related to that topic or that in some way illustrates your thesis. For example, if your essay shows that modern conveniences can be more trouble than they are worth, the following introduction with a story could be effective:

> The morning of my job interview, I woke up an hour earlier than usual and took special pains with my hair and makeup. I ate a light, sensible breakfast which managed to hit bottom despite the menagerie of winged insects fluttering around my stomach. I drove the parkway downtown, nervously biting my lower lip the whole way. I had to park three long blocks from the office building where the interview was to take place, and by the time I got to the building I was completely windblown. Breathless, I gasped my name to the receptionist, who explained that my interview would have to be postponed. The personnel director had never made it in. It seems her electricity was off, and she could not get her car out of the garage because the door was controlled by an electric opener. That's when I knew for sure that modern conveniences can be downright inconvenient.

✳ Use an Interesting Quotation

If someone has said something applicable to your thesis and said it particularly well, you can engage interest by quoting the remark. Just be sure that the quotation is interesting and not an overused expression like "better safe than sorry" or "the early bird gets the worm."

> Everyone seems to agree that we learn from our mistakes and that failure can be more instructive than success. As General Colin Powell has said, "There are no secrets to success. It is the result of preparation, hard work, learning from failure." Why, then, are students denied the opportunity to repeat courses without penalty? So we can profit from our mistakes, the administration should allow us to take courses three times and record the highest grade on our transcripts.

✳PROVIDE RELEVANT STATISTICS

Relevant statistics, particularly if they are surprising, can engage a reader. Just be sure that you note the source of the statistics you use, so your reader does not think you pulled them from the air.

> According to our campus newspaper, this college has spent $25 million for campus renovations in the last five years. During the same period, enrollment has dropped by 2,273 students, and 112 fewer people are employed here. These figures suggest that the administration cares more about buildings than people. It is time to reverse the trend and work to increase enrollment, faculty, and staff.

✳FIND SOME COMMON GROUND WITH YOUR READER

Identify a point of view or experience you and your reader share. Presenting this common ground in an introduction can create a bond between reader and writer. In the following introduction, the common ground is a shared school experience:

> Think back to when you were in high school. Remember the kids who caused all the trouble, the ones who disrupted the teacher and made it difficult for the rest of the class to learn? They were the students who did not want to be in school anyway and made things miserable for the students who did want to be there. Now imagine how much more learning would have occurred if the troublemakers had been allowed to quit school and get jobs. If we abolish compulsory attendance, everyone will be better off.

✳DESCRIBE SOMETHING

Description adds interest and liveliness to writing.

> At 5 feet 3 inches and 170 pounds, Mr. Daria looked like a meatball. His stringy black hair, always in need of a cut, kept sliding into his eyes, and his too-tight shirts would not stay tucked into his too-tight polyester pants. He wore the same sport coat everyday; it was easily identified by the grease splotch on the left lapel. Yes, Mr. Daria was considered a nerd by most of the student body, but to me he was the best history teacher on the planet.

✳BEGIN WITH THE THESIS AND THE POINTS YOU WILL DISCUSS

Sometimes the direct approach is the best. You can begin by stating your thesis and the main points you will discuss, like this:

> Carolyn Hotimsky is the best candidate for mayor for two reasons. First, as president of city council, she demonstrated leadership ability. Second, as chief investment counselor for First City Bank, she learned about sound fiscal management.

KEEP IT SHORT

If you are having trouble with something, it makes no sense to make it as long as possible. Thus, if your introduction is proving troublesome, just write your thesis and one or two other sentences, and get on with the rest of your writing. If all else fails, just write your thesis and go on to your first point to be developed.

WRITE IT LAST

If you cannot come up with a suitable introduction, go on to write the rest of your piece and then return to the introduction. With the rest of your writing drafted, you may find that an approach to your introduction comes to mind. However, if you skip your introduction, jot down a working thesis on scratch paper and check it periodically to be sure you do not stray off into unrelated areas.

TROUBLESHOOTING WITH A COMPUTER

If you use a computer, you may like the following techniques.

WINDOWING

If you cannot decide which of two or more approaches to use, execute the command that lets you divide your screen in half. Then try one approach to your introduction in one-half of the screen and another approach in the other half. Compare the two approaches and decide which works better.

TURN YOUR CONCLUSION INTO THE INTRODUCTION

Your last paragraph may work better as an introduction than as a conclusion. To find out, execute the command that allows you to move your conclusion to the beginning of your writing. With some fine-tuning, you may be able to turn the conclusion into a strong introduction. Of course, you will have to write a new conclusion, but that may prove easier than wrestling with the introduction.

USE THE INTERNET

These sites offer helpful information on writing introductions:

- The Nuts and Bolts of College Writing has examples of strong and weak introductions. Visit <nutsandbolts.washcoll.edu/beginning.html#opening>.
- George Mason University's online writing center offers a guide to introductions and conclusions at <www.gmu.edu/departments/writingcenter/handouts/introcon.html>.

CHAPTER SIX

"How Do I Back Up What I Say?"

You may be a warm, wonderful human being and as honest as they come, but no experienced reader will believe you unless you support your statements with proof and explanations. The suggestions in this chapter can help you back up what you say.

USE YOUR OWN EXPERIENCE

Your own life experiences can provide convincing evidence. Say, for example, that you are discussing problems created by computers, and you make the point that computers often contribute to procrastination. You might write a paragraph like the following, based on your own experience.

> Computers can be great time-wasters. The last time I sat down to write a paper, I found myself playing solitaire instead of drafting. The next thing I knew, an hour had gone by. I got myself back on task, but when I became stuck, I decided to check my e-mail. By the time I read and responded to five messages, another 20 minutes was lost. I tried to work on my paper again, but I was lured away by my favorite chatroom. I couldn't believe it when the clock in the corner of my screen showed that I had spent an hour discussing the latest Sheryl Crow CD. When I realized how much time I had wasted, I went straight back to my paper, but I was so tired that I know I didn't give it my best efforts. I probably would have done better had I used a pen and paper.

USE WHAT YOU OBSERVE

Your observations of the world can offer excellent support for ideas. Say you are discussing the trend to require volunteerism in high schools. Your observation of the volunteer work students do at local high schools could lead to this paragraph.

Students can learn a great deal when they are required to perform volunteer service. However, care must be taken with the kinds of activities they are allowed to engage in. At our local high school, students were at first involved in such worthy activities as volunteering in hospitals, purchasing groceries for elderly neighbors, and coaching youth soccer. Now they receive volunteer credit for such dubious activities as helping out in the school office during study hall, working on theater sets for the senior play, and selling programs at football games. I doubt very much is learned from such work.

TELL A STORY

Search your own experience for brief stories that can drive home your points. Consider this passage:

Distance running is an excellent sport for adolescents because even if they do not finish near the front of the pack, they can still feel good about themselves. Shaving a few seconds off an earlier time or completing a difficult course can be a genuine source of pride for a young runner.

Now notice how the addition of a brief story helps prove the point:

Distance running is an excellent sport for adolescents because even if they do not finish near the front of the pack, they can still feel good about themselves. Shaving a few seconds off an earlier time or completing a difficult course can be a genuine source of pride for a young runner. I remember a race I ran as a sophomore. I was recovering from a miserable cold and not in peak condition. Just after completing the first mile, I developed a cramp in my side. However, I was determined to finish, no matter how long it took me. Quarter mile by quarter mile, I ran rather haltingly. My chest was tight from lack of training because I had been sick, and my side hurt, but still I kept on. Eventually, I crossed the finish line, well back in the standings. However, I could not have been more proud of myself if I had won. I showed that I had what it took to finish, even though the going was tough.

DESCRIBE PEOPLE AND PLACES

Description creates vivid images that help the reader to see and hear the way you see and hear. It also adds interest and vitality to writing. Consider this passage:

The best teacher I ever had was Mrs. Suarez, who taught me algebra in the ninth grade. But even more than teaching me algebra, Mrs. Suarez showed me compassion during a very difficult time in my life. I will always be grateful for her understanding and encouragement when I needed them most.

In the ninth grade, I was a troubled teen, a victim of a difficult home life. Somehow Mrs. Suarez recognized my pain and approached me one day. . . .

Now notice the interest created with the addition of description:

The best teacher I ever had was Mrs. Suarez, who taught me algebra in the ninth grade. But even more than teaching me algebra, Mrs. Suarez showed me compassion during a very difficult time in my life. To look at this woman, a person would never guess what a caring nature she had. With wire-stiff hair teased and lacquered into a bouffant, Mrs. Suarez looked like a hard woman. Her face, heavily wrinkled, had a scary, witchlike quality that befit the shrill voice she used to reprimand 14-year-old sinners who neglected their homework. She always stood ramrod straight with her 120 pounds evenly distributed over her orthopedic shoes. Many a freshman has been frightened by a first look at this no-nonsense woman. However, appearances are, indeed, deceptive, for Mrs. Suarez was not the witch she looked to be. In fact, I will always be grateful for her understanding and encouragement when I needed them most.

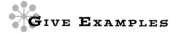

GIVE EXAMPLES

Nothing clarifies or proves a point like a well-chosen example. Examples can come from personal experience, observation, reading, research, or classroom experience. Assume you have stated that television commercials cause us to buy products we do not need. You could back up that point with examples you have observed, like this:

Television commercials often make people want products they do not need. For example, Tony the Tiger urges children to eat highly sugared cereal, while gorgeous, bikini-clad women romp on the beach, luring men to consume beer. Before Christmas, expensive toys based on the latest action hero are advertised relentlessly, until children are convinced they cannot survive without them. Of course, the worst offenders are the advertisers of hair dye, mascara, lipstick, perfume, and teeth-whiteners, who convince women they cannot be attractive without a drawer full of these products.

You could also take an example from personal experience (the time you went to a tax preparer because a commercial wrongly convinced you that you could not do your own taxes); you could draw an example from research (talk to others about unnecessary products they have purchased as a result of commercials); or you could cite an example you learned in the classroom (perhaps statistics on the number of people who buy a particular unnecessary product).

GIVE REASONS

Reasons help prove that something is true. Let's say that your point is that final examinations should be eliminated. These reasons could help prove your point: Finals create too much anxiety; they do not really show what a student knows;

placing considerable emphasis on one examination is not fair; some students test poorly. Here is how those reasons might appear in a paragraph:

Final examinations should be eliminated because they are not a sound educational practice. For one thing, these exams create too much anxiety among students. They worry so much about their performance that they lose sleep, stop eating, and show other signs of stress. Certainly, they cannot demonstrate what they know under such circumstances. They also cannot show what they really know because the tests cannot test all of a body of knowledge—just what the teacher wants to test. As a result, some of what a student knows may never be asked for. Furthermore, if the test is poorly constructed (and many of them are), students may further be kept from demonstrating their real learning. Then there is the fact that many students are poor test-takers. They may know the material just fine but be incapable of demonstrating their knowledge because they have never mastered the art of test-taking.

✳ SHOW SIMILARITIES OR DIFFERENCES

Assume you are writing about ways to improve the quality of life in nursing homes, and you make the point that nursing homes should allow residents to have pets. The following paragraph shows how you can back up your point by citing similarities.

Because nursing homes have long recognized the value of having young children visit residents, preschool classes are often invited to spend time in the facilities. Allowing the residents to have pets would be similarly beneficial. Just as the children do, the pets would provide companionship for the residents and give them an opportunity to express affection. Also, just as it does with children, the interaction with pets would provide intellectual stimulation and an opportunity to forget about infirmities. Of course, in one respect, pets are better than children: they do not have to go home at the end of the day because they already are home and can continue to make life better for residents.

Now assume that you want to argue that having pets in nursing homes is *not* a good idea. Showing differences can help you back up your point.

Some people claim that having pets in nursing homes would be beneficial in the same way that having preschoolers there is beneficial. This is not true. First, children will not add cost to a nursing home or its residents. Their parents feed them and take care of medical expenses, but the residents or nursing home would have to assume these expenses for pets. Also, because children are supervised by their teachers while in the facility, residents need not watch them very closely. Pets, on the other hand, need to be restrained from entering the rooms of residents who do not want to be near them. Since many residents cannot supervise the animals all the time, an already overburdened staff would have even more responsibility. Finally, children go home at the end of the day, but pets stay and require ongoing care, which can drain nursing home resources.

✳ EXPLAIN CAUSES OR EFFECTS

If you are writing about sex education in schools and make the point that it should be mandatory, you can back up this point by citing the positive effects of sex education, like this:

> Sex education's most obvious benefit is increased knowledge. Since it is unlikely that sexually active teens will start to abstain, increased knowledge about birth control will prevent unwanted pregnancy. Furthermore, the same knowledge can help teens protect themselves against sexually transmitted disease. When fewer teens become pregnant, more of them will stay in school and thus will not fall victim to unemployment, drugs, and crime. When more teens protect themselves against sexually transmitted diseases, fewer will die.

If you want to emphasize the need for sex education by citing the pressure on teenagers to become sexually active, you might explain what causes teenagers to become sexually active, like this:

> One reason teenagers are sexually active at a younger age is that they are bombarded by sexual messages. On MTV, videos are populated with women wearing next to nothing; men and women are touching, groping, and grinding in sexually provocative ways. On the radio, rock lyrics glorify teen sex as healthy rebellion and a sign of independence. Movies, too, send sexual messages. Sex scenes and nudity are frequent in PG-13 movies and are standard fare in R-rated movies that teens get into with no trouble at all.

To discover causes, ask yourself, "Why does this happen?" The answers may provide your details. Similarly, to discover effects, ask yourself, "After this happens, then what?" The answers may provide details as well. For example, ask, "Why do teenagers engage in sex?" and you might get the answer, "To be more like an adult." The desire to be mature then becomes a cause. Ask yourself, "After sex education courses are offered, then what?" If you get the answer, "Teenagers learn safe sex practices," you have an effect of sex education.

✳ EXPLAIN HOW SOMETHING IS MADE OR DONE

Assume you are discussing simple things people can do to combat prejudice. If you make the point that people do not have to put up with racial, ethnic, or sexist humor, you might back up that point by explaining how a person can deal with such humor, like this:

> Many people do not know how to respond when they are told a racial, ethnic, or sexist joke, so they smile or laugh politely, even though they feel uncomfortable. A better approach is to say something simple, such as, "I don't find such jokes

funny." Then, you can quickly turn the conversation to some neutral topic. If the joke was told to several people, and you do not want to embarrass the speaker, draw him or her aside later and say, "I'm sure you did not mean to, but you made me very uncomfortable when you told your joke." Both of these approaches let the speaker know that hurtful jokes are not universally welcome.

✳ EXPLAIN WHAT WOULD HAPPEN IF YOUR VIEW WERE NOT ADOPTED

Say, for example that you are arguing for the passage of a tax levy to fund the building of a new high school. To help make your point, you can explain what would happen if the levy did *not* pass, like this:

Without the passage of the levy, funds would not be available to finance a new high school. Yet without the high school, our children will suffer. The current building is too small, and enrollment is projected to increase over the next five years. Thus, classes will be seriously overcrowded. Furthermore, the current building lacks an auditorium, making it impossible to have a theater program. The lack of an auditorium also means assemblies and band concerts must be held in the gym, where the acoustics are poor and the seats are uncomfortable. Most worrisome is the fact that the renovations required in the existing building, including asbestos removal, a new roof, and updated heating system, will cost almost as much as building a new school. If we spend money on these renovations, the children will reap no benefits, the way they would with a new building.

✳ CONSIDER OPPOSING VIEWS

Think about the view of those who disagree with you. You can acknowledge a compelling point and offer your counterargument. For example, if you were arguing in favor of warning labels on CDs with sexually explicit lyrics, you could write the following.

People against warning labels cite the "forbidden fruit" argument. They say that young people will be encouraged to buy music with the labels, expressly because they are being warned away from them. To some extent this is true. However, the labels will still provide a guideline for parents who want to buy music for their children. They will also create an atmosphere of acceptability. Although young people may ignore them, the labels still send a message that some things are more appropriate than others for teenagers. This atmosphere is an improvement over the current "anything goes" climate that sends the message that teens can buy and do whatever they please. Down the road, stores may even refuse to sell labeled music to those under 21.

USE MATERIAL FROM OUTSIDE SOURCES

Statistics, facts, quotations, and ideas from outside sources can provide important support for many topics. These sources can include your textbooks and class lectures, newspapers, magazines, and sources you discover in the library or on the Internet. You should judge the credibility of any material from outside sources according to the guidelines on page 170.

TROUBLESHOOTING WITH A COMPUTER

These strategies can help back up your ideas.

USE THE WORD COUNT FEATURE

Sometimes, the number of words that develop an idea can be a clue to how well developed the idea is. Most word processing programs will tally the number of words you have written. If you are using Microsoft Word, highlight the section discussing the idea in question. Then, go to "Tools" on the toolbar and then "Word Count." You will be given the number of words in the highlighted section. Although word count is not by itself a reliable indication of sufficient support, it does offer one measure for you to consider.

E-MAIL A RELIABLE READER FOR IDEAS

If a passage of your draft needs more back up, e-mail that section to a reliable reader and ask for suggestions.

USE THE INTERNET

You can use the Internet for research to find quotations, statistics, facts, and informed opinions to help back up your points.

- Type your topic into your favorite search engine, to locate relevant web pages.
- Check Vocabula Review's site at <www.vocabula.com/VRlinks.htm> to locate magazines, journals, and news sources that can be helpful.
- Visit <www.findarticles.com> to locate magazine articles about your topic.

If you use material from the Internet (or any other source), be sure to document that material according to the guidelines explained in Chapter 29.

CHAPTER SEVEN

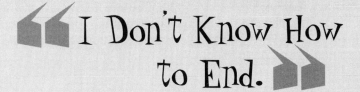

" I Don't Know How to End. "

I magine that you go to the movies and pay $8.00 to see the latest action film. The beginning is wonderful—you're on the edge of your seat; the middle is very exciting—you're completely caught up in the plot. Then the ending comes—and it's awful. When you walk out of the theater, you probably do not talk about how good the beginning and middle were. Instead, you probably complain about how bad the ending was. Why? Because endings form the last impression, the one that is most remembered.

Your conclusion forms your reader's final impression. If you write a weak conclusion, no matter how strong the rest of your essay is, your reader will feel let down. If you have trouble ending your writing, try the strategies in this chapter.

✳ EXPLAIN THE SIGNIFICANCE OF YOUR MAIN POINT

Ideas in the conclusion are emphasized because of their placement at the end, where they are most likely to be remembered. Therefore, the conclusion can be a good place to state the significance of your point. For example, say your essay tells the story of the time you were cut from the junior high school basketball team. Your conclusion can explain the significance of the event:

> Because being cut from the team shattered my self-esteem at such a young age, I have struggled all my life with feelings of inadequacy. I have doubted my ability because the coach, whose judgment I trusted, told me that I didn't have what it takes.

✳ PROVIDE A HELPFUL SUMMARY

Summarizing your main points is a service to your reader if you have written a long essay or one with complex ideas. After reading a long or complicated writing, a reader will appreciate a review. However, if your essay is short or if the ideas are easily grasped, a summary is a boring rehash of previously covered material.

✳ EXPLAIN THE CONSEQUENCES OF IGNORING YOUR THESIS

If you are writing to persuade your reader to think or act a certain way, you can close by explaining what would happen if your reader did not follow your recommendation. Assume, for example, that you are writing to convince your reader that a drug education program should be instituted in the local elementary school. After giving your reasons, you could close like this:

> If we do not have a drug education program in the earliest grades, we miss the opportunity to influence our children when they are the most impressionable. If we miss this opportunity to influence them when they are young and responsive to adult pressure, we run the risk of losing our children to powerful peer pressure to experiment with drugs.

✳ CONCLUDE WITH A POINT YOU WANT TO EMPHASIZE

Anything placed at the end is emphasized. Therefore, you can conclude with your most important point, the one you want underscored in your reader's mind. For example, if you are explaining the differences between child-rearing practices of today and those of 50 years ago, you could end like this:

> The most telling difference between child-rearing practices of today and those of 50 years ago is that today's parents are less rigid. Unlike the parents of 50 years ago, they are less concerned with doing everything on schedule and by the book. Babies are not forced to eat and sleep at specific times but may do so when they are hungry and sleepy. Today's parents trust their instincts more than they trust the child-care book used by parents of the past. Thus, they are more likely to do what they think is right and not worry about what the "authorities" say.

✳ RESTATE YOUR THESIS FOR EMPHASIS

Repetition is effective for judicious emphasis, but repetition is boring and annoying if it is unnecessary. Thus, if you decide to close by restating your thesis, be sure the restatement is effective emphasis rather than boring repetition. Also, avoid restating in the same language you used previously. Restate the thesis a *new* way.

✳ Suggest a Course of Action

You can conclude by stating a remedy to a problem your essay discusses, or by calling your reader to action. For example, if your essay explains the reason for declining enrollment at your school, you can suggest a course of action in the conclusion:

> The reasons for our declining enrollment are complex, but the solution to the problem is clear. First, we should hire a recruitment specialist and charge that person with aggressively seeking new students. At the same time, we should begin a marketing campaign, complete with local television and radio spots, to attract area people so they attend school here rather than out of state. Finally, we should hire a marketing firm to discover what potential students are seeking and try to meet those desires. Yes, these measures are expensive, but the money will be well spent if we can return enrollment figures to their previous high levels.

✳ Ask a Question

You can leave your reader thinking about your thesis if you close with a suitable question, as exemplified in this conclusion for an essay arguing against raising the speed limit on state routes.

> If the speed limit is raised, truckers would save money, as would those who ship their goods on trucks. And while studies do not support the contention that the higher speed limit will mean more accidents, they suggest that the accidents that do occur would involve more fatalities. Do we really want to save money but lose lives?

✳ Look to the Future

Sometimes you can write an effective conclusion by looking ahead to the time beyond your essay. Say your essay explains the benefits and drawbacks of purchasing goods on the Internet. You could close by looking to the future, like this:

> Although e-commerce has become increasingly popular over the last five years, the next five years will show a marked decline as people return to traditional stores. The novelty of online shopping will wear off as consumers admit to the difficulties of shopping for clothing and gifts they cannot touch, try on, and examine first hand. Increased shipping costs will render online shopping too expensive, and fears about electronic security breaches (reasonable or not) will deter many consumers. Finally, consumers often miss the social and recreational aspects of shopping and will return to traditional stores for the simple human interaction they offer.

✳ COMBINE APPROACHES

You can combine any two or more approaches to create a strong conclusion. For example, you can summarize main points and then make a recommendation, or you can restate your thesis and then ask a question.

✳ KEEP IT SHORT

If you have trouble with your conclusion, keep it short. Although you do not want to end abruptly, do not take something that is a problem and stretch it out longer than necessary. A perfectly effective conclusion can be only one or two sentences.

 TROUBLESHOOTING WITH A COMPUTER

You can try the next strategies if you compose at the computer.

USE E-MAIL

E-mail your draft *without* a conclusion to three reliable readers, and ask each one what he or she suggests for an approach to the ending. You might like one or more of the ideas.

DIVIDE YOUR SCREEN

Divide your screen in half and write two conclusions, using two different approaches, each in its own screen. Compare the two approaches and decide which works better.

USE THE INTERNET

George Mason University's Writing Center offers an online handout on introductions and conclusions that explains concluding strategies writers should avoid. Visit <www.gmu.edu/departments/writingcenter/handouts/introcon.html>.

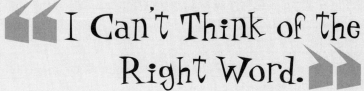

CHAPTER EIGHT

"I Can't Think of the Right Word."

Y ou're writing along, and just as your confidence begins to surge—wham! You're stuck because you can't think of the right word. You try all the usual techniques—chewing on the end of your pencil to squeeze the word into the tip, rubbing your forehead to massage the word into your brain, and staring at the computer screen to will the word to appear—but nothing helps. Soon it's a matter of pride, and you refuse to budge until you think of the word that's lurking annoyingly just at the tip of your tongue. The next thing you know, 15 minutes have passed, you have made no progress, and you are frustrated.

The next time the word you need escapes you, avoid frustration with the techniques in this chapter.

WRITE IN A NATURAL STYLE

You may be straining for an overly "sophisticated" style, a style you think will impress the reader. As a result, words escape you because you are seeking ones that were never a natural part of your vocabulary in the first place. Return to a more natural style, and words should come more easily.

Unnatural: Attempting to ruminate her morning nourishment while simultaneously communicating the events that transpired, Emma began to choke on her victuals.

More natural: Trying to tell what happened at the same time she was eating breakfast, Emma began to choke.

Use ITTS

ITTS stands for *"I'm trying to say."* When you cannot find the right word, stop for a moment and say to yourself, "I'm trying to say _____ ." Imagine yourself explaining what you mean to a friend and fill in the blank with the word or words you would speak to that friend. Then write the word or words in your draft. You may use several words or even a sentence to fill in the blank when originally you were only seeking a single word. That's fine.

Substitute a Phrase or a Sentence for a Troublesome Word

If you cannot take one path, then take an alternate route to your destination: If you cannot think of the right word, try using a phrase or a whole sentence to express your idea instead.

Ask Around

If you cannot think of the word that is on the tip of your tongue, then ask around. To anyone who will listen, just say, "Hey, what's the word for ____?" Writers are always glad to help each other.

Freewrite for Three Minutes

You may not be able to think of the right word because you are not certain about what you want to say. To clarify your thinking, try three minutes of freewriting, focusing on the idea you want the word to convey. (Freewriting is explained on page 23.) After the freewriting, try again to come up with the word. You may be able to do so with a better understanding of what you want to express.

Skip the Problem and Return to It Later

When you are drafting, never let any one trouble spot stop your progress. If after a minute you cannot think of the right word, then leave a blank space and push on. You can return to consider the problem again when you revise. When you return, the word may surface, and the problem will be solved. If not, you can try the other strategies in this chapter.

Use Simple, Specific Words

Some people have trouble finding the right words because they think good writing uses words like *bumptious, egregious, panacea, parsimonious,* and *pusillanimous.* The truth is that good writing is clear, simple, and specific. You do not need the high-flown, 50-dollar words. Instead of *parsimonious,* use *stingy.*

Use the Thesaurus and Dictionary Wisely

The thesaurus and dictionary are excellent tools for writers seeking the right word. In fact, you may want to invest in a hardback and paperback version of each of these resources. Keep the hardbacks on your writing desk, and carry the paperbacks around with you. A word of caution: Be sure you understand the connotation (secondary meaning) of any word you draw from these sources. For example, *skinny* and *lean* may mean the same thing on one level, but because of their connotations, a person would rather be called *lean* than *skinny.* If you do not understand the connotations of a word, you can misuse it or offend your reader.

TROUBLE SHOOTING WITH A COMPUTER

Try the next strategies if you compose at the computer.

Use a Thesaurus Program

Many word processing programs come with a built-in thesaurus, or you can purchase an add-on thesaurus. Such a program can be handy, but be sure you understand the meaning of any word you take from this source.

Learn a Word a Day

Visit one of these sites to have a new word and its meaning e-mailed to you each day:

- <www.wordsmith.org>
- <www.vocabvitamins.com>
- <www.m-w.com>

USE THE INTERNET

- If you like visual representations, check the visual thesaurus at <www.visual thesaurus.com/online/index.html>. This site uses maps to show the relationships between words and meanings.

- For an online thesaurus, visit the Mirriam Webster site at <www.m-w.com>.

- Take Our Word for It is a webzine about words. To see what it offers, visit <www.takeourword.com>.

- For vocabulary building help, visit <www.wordfocus.com>.

Part III

A Troubleshooting Guide to Revising

First drafts *always* have problems—that's why they are also called **rough drafts.** However, even the most troubled first draft gives you material to shape, refine, and improve. When you evaluate your first draft to determine what to change and when you make those changes, you are **revising.** To revise, consider your content, organization, and expression of ideas. Do not worry about grammar, spelling, capitalization, or punctuation just yet.

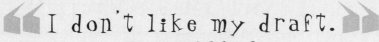

TROUBLESHOOTING STRATEGIES

I don't like my draft.

Have you tried these?

❏ Walking away **(p. 74)**   ❏ Listening to the draft **(p. 75)**
❏ Sharing **(p. 74)**   ❏ Making two changes **(p. 75)**

I don't know what to change.

Have you tried these?

❏ Walking away **(p. 78)**   ❏ Typing **(p. 80)**
❏ Thinking like a reader **(p. 79)**   ❏ Revising in stages **(p. 80)**

I'm not a good collaborator.

Have you tried these?

❏ Choosing readers   ❏ Asking for ways to
   carefully **(p. 85)**   revise **(p. 87)**
❏ Giving guidance **(p. 85)** ❏ Evaluating responses **(p. 87)**

I need to reorganize.

Have you tried these?

❏ Using topic sentences **(p. 89)**   ❏ Repeating key words **(p. 90)**
❏ Using transitions **(p. 90)**   ❏ Using synonyms **(p. 90)**

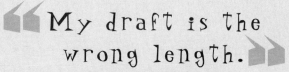
My draft is the wrong length.

Have you tried these?

- ❏ Showing after telling **(p. 94)**
- ❏ Sharing your draft **(p. 95)**
- ❏ Checking your thesis **(p. 96)**
- ❏ Outlining **(p. 99)**

My draft is boring.

Have you tried these?

- ❏ Using specific words **(p. 102)**
- ❏ Adding dialogue **(p. 104)**
- ❏ Adding description **(p. 104)**
- ❏ Telling a story **(p. 104)**

My writing sounds choppy.

Have you tried these?

- ❏ Varying sentence openers **(p. 107)**
- ❏ Moving transitions **(p. 108)**
- ❏ Combining sentences **(p. 108)**
- ❏ Using parallelism **(p. 109)**

CHAPTER NINE

"I Thought My Draft Was Better Than This."

You've just placed the final period at the end of the last sentence of your first draft, and you're feeling proud of yourself. So you lean back, put your feet up on the desk, and start to reread the masterpiece. However, as you read, your masterpiece doesn't seem nearly as good as you thought it was. Does this mean you have to start over? Probably not. Instead, try some of the suggestions in this chapter.

BE REALISTIC

Remember, a first draft is called a *rough* draft because your first attempt is supposed to have problems—even lots of them. Do not expect too much too soon. Instead, realize that your first pass is bound to be rough, roll up your sleeves, and get in there and revise.

WALK AWAY

Before deciding about the quality of your draft, put it aside for a while to regain your objectivity. The longer you stay away, the better; but walk away for at least several hours—for a day if you have the time. When you return to your draft and reread it, you may discover potential that you overlooked previously.

SHARE YOUR DRAFT

Sometimes writers are too hard on themselves. Instead of recognizing the potential in their drafts, they see only the rough spots. As a result, they become frustrated and start over unnecessarily. Before deciding about the quality of your draft, share it with several people whose judgment you trust. Ask what they like and what they want to hear more about. Your readers' comments may reveal how much potential your draft has. (For more on reader response, see Chapter 11.)

Listen to Your Draft

Your draft may seem worse than it is if it is messy or written in sloppy handwriting or written in pencil or written on paper ripped out of a spiral notebook. In short, the appearance of the draft may affect your evaluation of it. To judge the worth of your draft more reliably, ask someone to read it to you. You may hear sections that are stronger than you realized.

Identify Two Changes That Will Improve Your Draft

Identify two changes that will make your draft better, and you may recognize how much potential your draft has. If you think it will help you judge your draft better, make those changes and *then* decide how you feel about your draft.

Write a Second Draft without Looking at the First

Writing a second draft without looking at the first is often successful because you manage to retain the best parts of the first draft, eliminate the weakest parts, and add some new, effective material. The key is to avoid checking the first draft while writing the second.

Do Not Despair if You Must Start Over

Often we must discover what we do *not* want to do before we discover what we *do* want to do; sometimes we must learn what we *cannot* do before we are clear about what we *can* do. If you must begin again, do not be discouraged. Your first draft was not a waste of your time—it was groundwork that paved the way for your most recent effort.

Try to Salvage Something

If you must begin again, try to salvage something. Perhaps you can use the same approach to your introduction, or some of your examples, or one main idea. While it is tempting to rip the draft to shreds and begin anew, you may not have to begin at square one. Some of your work may be usable in your new draft.

Do the Best You Can with What You Have

Yes, writers start over all the time, but writers do not usually have an unlimited amount of time to work within. At some point you must force yourself to push forward, even if you are not completely comfortable with the status of your first draft. When time is running out, do the best you can with what you have and be satisfied that you have met your deadline.

TROUBLESHOOTING WITH A COMPUTER

Computers can help writers revise efficiently. Consider the following strategies.

Evaluate a Print Copy of Your Draft

Computer screens display a small portion of your draft, making it hard to get a good overview. To decide about the strengths and weaknesses of your draft, print out a copy and read that.

Save Your Scraps

You may be tempted to hit the delete key, especially if you decide to start over, but resist the impulse. Save your first draft and any material you decide to omit in a separate "scraps" file. If you change your mind later and want to use the material, you will have it. If you are using MS Word, you can save every version of your draft by clicking on "File" and then "Versions."

Use the Internet

For some questions to help you evaluate your draft, visit the Paradigm Online Writing Assistant at <www.powa.org>. Click on "Revising" and then on "Global and Local Perspectives."

EXAMINING A DRAFT

The following is a first draft of paragraph 5 of "The Uniform Solution" on page 16. To understand that a first draft can have problems but still be full of potential, read the paragraph and then compare it to the final version. You will notice that the final version reads much better and backs up its point better.

People who want school uniforms say that having such uniforms will save parents money because they will not have to buy expensive clothes. However, not everything should be about money. Uniforms probably are a cost saving device for parents, but the drawbacks overshadow the good aspect of the amount of money parents can save. An important drawback is the fact that students lose the freedom to express themselves through their clothing.

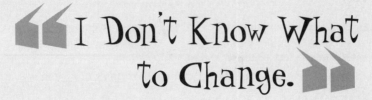"I Don't Know What to Change."

Good news! You finished your first draft, and you are ready to dig in and make all those changes that will improve your writing. So you read your draft—but wait a minute—everything seems fine. *You* understand what you mean; everything seems clear and well developed to *you*. In fact, you can't figure out what changes to make and what all the revision fuss is about. The suggestions in this chapter can help.

WALK AWAY

Before revising, put your draft aside for a day, or longer if possible. Getting away from your writing gives you a chance to regain your objectivity so that when you return to revise, you can identify necessary changes more readily.

CONSTRUCT A READER PROFILE

As the writer, you may have no trouble figuring out what you meant when you wrote all those words, but that does not guarantee that your reader will have an easy time of it. To revise successfully, view your draft as the reader and make changes to meet your reader's needs. Different readers will place different demands on a writer. For example, assume you are writing to convince your reader to vote for a school levy that will increase property taxes. If your audience is someone with children in the school system, explaining that the additional revenue will go toward enhancing the art and music curriculum may be sufficiently persuasive. However, if your reader is a childless retired person on a fixed income, this argument may not be very convincing. Instead, you may need to explain that better schools will cause the reader's home to increase in value so the resale price is higher.

To evaluate your detail from your reader's point of view, construct a reader profile by answering the following 10 questions:

1. How much education does my reader have?
2. What are my reader's age, sex, race, nationality, and religion?
3. What are my reader's occupation and socioeconomic level?
4. What part of the country does my reader live in? Does my reader live in an urban or rural area?
5. What is my reader's political affiliation?
6. How familiar is my reader with my topic?
7. What does my reader need to know to appreciate my point of view?
8. How resistant will my reader be to my point of view?
9. How hard will I have to work to create interest in my topic?
10. Does my reader have any special hobbies or interests or concerns that will affect how my essay is viewed? Is my reader chiefly concerned with money? career? the environment? society? religion? family?

After answering these questions, review your draft with an eye toward providing detail suited to your reader's unique makeup.

Think Like Your Reader

Asking the following questions as you study your draft can help you think like your reader and identify necessary changes:

1. Is there any place where my reader might lose interest?
2. Is there any place where my reader might not understand what I mean?
3. Is there any place where my reader is not likely to be convinced of the truth of my topic sentence or thesis?

Describe Your Draft Paragraph by Paragraph

Describing your draft paragraph by paragraph can help you analyze its strengths and weaknesses. To do this, summarize the content of paragraph 1; then explain how that paragraph meets your audience's needs and how it helps you achieve your purpose for writing. Next, summarize the content of paragraph 2; then explain how that paragraph meets your audience's needs and your purpose. Continue in this fashion until you have described each paragraph. Read your description to identify points that stray from your thesis, ideas that need more development, and paragraphs that fail to meet a reader's needs or your purpose.

Type Your Draft

If you handwrote your draft, type it, print it out, and then read it over. Problems you overlook in your own handwriting are more apparent in type because the copy resembles printed material rather than your own handiwork. As a result, it can be easier to be objective about the writing. Also, some mistakes may leap out at you. For example, a paragraph that ran the better part of a page in your handwritten copy may be only three typed lines—a visual signal that more detail may be needed.

Listen to Your Draft

Often, you can hear problems that you overlook visually. For this reason, you should read your draft out loud at least once. Be sure to go slowly and be careful to read *exactly* what is on the page. If you read quickly, you are likely to read what you *meant* to write rather than what you actually *did* write.

Some writers do well if they read their drafts into a tape recorder. Then they play back the tape to listen for problems. Still other writers prefer to have other people read their drafts to them. Sometimes, another person's voice helps the writer pick up on problems.

Underline Main Points

One way to determine if you have supported your points is to go through your draft and underline every main idea. Then check to see what appears after each underlined point. If one underlined point is immediately followed by another underlined point, you have not supported a main idea. Similarly, if an underlined idea is followed by only one or two sentences, you should consider whether you have enough support. For strategies for supporting points, see Chapter 6.

Outline Your Draft after Writing It

A good way to determine if your ideas follow logically one to the next is to outline your draft *after* writing it. If you have points that do not fit into the outline at the appropriate spots, you have discovered an organization problem.

Revise in Stages

When you revise, you have a great deal to consider. To consider it all, revise in stages, using one of the following patterns.

Easy to Hard

First make all the easy changes, take a break, and then make the more difficult changes. Take a break whenever you become tired or when you get stuck. Making the easy changes first helps you build enough momentum to carry you through the harder changes.

Hard to Easy

Make some of your more difficult changes, take a break, make some more of your difficult changes, take another break, and continue with the harder changes, taking breaks as needed. When you have finished the more difficult changes, tackle the easier ones. Some writers like the psychological lift that comes from getting the hard changes out of the way.

Paragraph by Paragraph

Revise your first paragraph until it is as perfect as you can make it, and then go on to the next paragraph. Proceed paragraph by paragraph, taking a break after every paragraph or two.

Content–Organization–Effective Expression

First make all your content changes: adequate detail, relevant detail, specific detail, clarity, and suitable introduction and conclusion. Then take a break and check the organization: logical order of ideas, effective thesis, and clear topic sentences. Take another break and revise for sentence effectiveness: effective word choice, smooth flow, helpful transitions.

SHARE YOUR INTRODUCTION AND CONCLUSION

To judge the effectiveness of your introduction and conclusion, type up these parts separately, and give them to two or three people to read. Ask them whether they would be interested in reading something that opened and closed with these paragraphs.

SHARE YOUR DRAFT

To help them decide what and how to revise, writers often ask reliable readers to read their drafts and make suggestions. If you want to consider the opinions of readers when you make revision decisions, refer to the strategies in Chapter 11.

✳ PRETEND TO BE SOMEONE ELSE

To be more objective about your work, pretend you are someone else. Read your draft as the judge of a contest who will award you $10,000 for a prize-winning essay. Or become the editor of a magazine who is deciding what changes to make in the draft before publishing the piece. Or read as your worst enemy, someone who loves to find fault with your work.

✳ USE A REVISING CHECKLIST

Some writers like to use a revising checklist like the following one. The checklist keeps you from overlooking some of the revision concerns. In addition, you can combine this checklist with reader response by asking a reliable reader to apply the checklist to your draft. (The page numbers in parentheses refer to helpful pages in this book.)

Content

1. Does your writing have a clear thesis, either stated or implied, that accurately presents your focus? (page 35)
2. Does every point in your writing clearly relate to that thesis? (page 15)
3. Are all your generalizations, including your thesis, adequately supported? (page 14)
4. Are all your points well suited to your audience and purpose? (pages 6 and 8.)
5. Have you avoided stating the obvious? (page 103)
6. Does your introduction create interest in your topic? (page 52)
7. Does your conclusion provide a satisfying ending? (page 63)

Organization

1. Do your ideas follow logically one to the next? (page 15)
2. Do your paragraphs follow logically one to the next? (page 15)
3. Do the details in each paragraph relate to the topic sentence? (page 15)
4. Have you used transitions to show how ideas relate to each other? (page 90)

Expression

1. When you read your work aloud, does everything sound all right? (page 75)
2. Have you avoided wordiness? (page 99)
3. Have you eliminated clichés (overworked expressions)? (page 103)
4. Have you used specific words? (page 102)
5. Did you use a variety of sentence openers? (page 107)

6. Have you used the active voice? (page 103)

7. Have you used action verbs rather than forms of *be?* (page 103)

8. Have you used parallel structures? (page 109)

Trust Your Instincts

When your instincts tell you that something is wrong, assume you have a problem. Even if you cannot give the problem a name, and even if you are not yet sure what change should be made, you have identified something that needs to be reworked. Most of the time, a writer's instincts are correct.

Do Not Edit Prematurely

Sometimes writers have trouble deciding what to change because they get bogged down checking commas, spelling, fragments, and the like. However, concerns such as these are matters of correctness and are best dealt with later, during editing. During revision, focus on content, organization, and effective expression. Do not be distracted by editing concerns too early in the writing process.

TROUBLESHOOTING WITH A COMPUTER

The following computer tips may help you decide what changes to make.

Study a Print Copy of Your Draft

When you view the text on the screen, you see small portions at a time, so you don't get a good overview of your writing.

Do Not Be Fooled by Appearances

Word-processed material looks very professional because it is so neat and well formatted. Do not let the appearance of your draft fool you into thinking that no changes are needed.

Use the Find and Replace Command

If you tend to overuse certain words, use MS Word's Find and Replace command to check how many times you have used those words. For example, if you overuse "very," type "very" into *both* the "Find" and "Replace" boxes. Then click on "Replace All," and Word will count the number of times you have used that word to help you judge whether you have used it too much. (Nothing will be replaced.)

KEEP YOUR READER PROFILE AND REVISION CHECKLIST AS FILES

If you keep your reader profile and revision checklist as files, you can consult them each time you revise. If your computer allows you to split your screen, place the checklist or profile in a window to refer to as you revise.

USE THE INTERNET

For helpful information on how to revise, visit this University of Texas website: <www.utexas.edu/student/utlc/handouts/1234.html>.

EXAMINING A DRAFT

The following is an early version of paragraph 3 of "The Uniform Solution" on page 16. If the author asked you to be a reliable reader and react to this paragraph, what would you tell her?

Requiring students to wear uniforms takes away their right to express themselves through their clothes in a way that promotes their individuality. Theres not much opportunity as it is for individuality in schools because everything is about conforming. Schools have to have as much sameness as possible in their classes and rules or else their would be chaos. Its important to let students at least express themselves in their clothing and get away from the conformity.

CHAPTER ELEVEN

"Is It Cheating if Someone Helps Me?"

O f course it's cheating if someone else writes all or part of your paper or if you copy someone else's work and turn it in as your own. But that doesn't mean other people can't lend a hand. In fact, when they revise, writers often seek feedback and ideas from other people. That's why you so often hear a writer say, "Read this and tell me what you think." Because the opinion of readers is so valuable to writers, this chapter explains strategies for securing helpful reader response.

CHOOSE YOUR READERS CAREFULLY

Be sure the people who read your work know the qualities of effective writing. A person who has never taken a writing course may not be a good choice. Also be sure that your readers are comfortable giving constructive criticism; do not use someone who is reluctant to tell you if something is wrong.

GIVE YOUR READERS A LEGIBLE DRAFT

Make your reader's job as easy as possible. If necessary, print out or write a fresh, clear copy of your draft so they can easily read your work.

GIVE YOUR READERS GUIDANCE

If you have specific concerns about your draft, mention them and ask your readers to speak to those points. As an alternative, give your readers a questionnaire, like this one:

Reader Response Questionnaire

1. Can you easily tell what the thesis is? If so, what is that thesis?

   _____

   _____

2. Are you interested in reading about this thesis? Why or why not?

   _____

   _____

3. What do you like best about this essay?

   _____

   _____

4. Do any points go unproven or unsupported? If so, which ones?

   _____

   _____

5. Is there anything you do not understand? If so, what?

   _____

   _____

6. Does the order of ideas make sense? If not, explain the problem.

   _____

   _____

7. Does any detail stray from the thesis? If so, what?

   _____

   _____

8. Does the introduction engage your interest? Why or why not?

   _____

   _____

9. Is the conclusion satisfying? Why or why not?

   _____

   _____

10. What advice do you have that was not covered by the previous questions?

   _____

   _____

✳ GET MORE THAN ONE OPINION

Ask two or three reliable readers to respond to your draft, and then look for consensus. When multiple readers agree, chances are they are right. If a reader makes a comment you are unsure about, ask another reader to speak to that same point so you can have another opinion.

✳ ASK FOR SPECIFIC REVISION STRATEGIES

Readers should do more than point out problems; they should also suggest ways to solve those problems. Instead of "paragraph 2 needs detail," a reader should say, "Paragraph 2 needs more detail. Perhaps you could add two examples of how schools reward conformity."

✳ ASK READERS TO POINT OUT STRENGTHS as WELL as WEAKNESSES

To revise effectively, you need a sense of your draft's strengths *and* weaknesses, so ask your readers what they like best about your draft and why.

✳ EVALUATE RESPONSES CAREFULLY

Do not assume your readers are always correct. Weigh out their responses carefully. If you are unsure about the value of a response, ask you instructor or a writing center tutor. If you need clarification, ask your readers why they responded as they did.

 TROUBLESHOOTING WITH A COMPUTER

If you like to compose and revise at the computer, you may like the next strategies.

E-MAIL YOUR DRAFT

E-Mail your draft to reliable readers to secure their reactions. If you want them to respond to particular sections of the draft, boldface those sections and ask your readers to pay particular attention to those parts. Many word processing programs allow inserting comments on the draft. For MS Word, highlight the text to comment on, click "Insert" and then "Comment." A window appears at the bottom of the screen with comments that have already been made and the initials of the person who made the comment. Type your comments next to your initials and click on "Close." Yellow highlighting on the draft will signal that a comment has been made.

USE THE INTERNET

For information on how to give useful feedback to other writers, see the University of Wisconsin—Madison's website at <www.wise.edu/writing/Handbook/PeerReviews.html>.

EXAMINING A DRAFT

In Chapter 10 (see page 84), you looked at this early version of paragraph 3 of "The Uniform Solution" on page 16:

Requiring students to wear uniforms takes away their right to express themselves through their clothes in a way that promotes their individuality. Theres not much opportunity as it is for individuality in schools because everything is about conforming. Schools have to have as much sameness as possible in their classes and rules or else their would be chaos. Its important to let students at least express themselves in their clothing and get away from the conformity.

The writer asked a classmate to read and react to her first draft. Below is that reader's response to paragraph 3 above. Did the essay's author address her reader's concerns in the final draft? Explain.

Rachel,
This paragraph makes it clear that you are against uniforms because they promote conformity and eliminate an opportunity for self-expression. I think that's an important point to make. It's really your most important point. However, I wish you would back up what you say. How is everything about conformity? Why do students need self-expression?

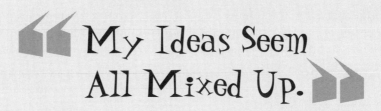

CHAPTER TWELVE

"My Ideas Seem All Mixed Up."

et's say you finish your draft, and you're feeling confident until you read it over—or a reliable reader does—and you discover that your ideas do not seem connected to each other. Everything is a jumble. Does this mean your ideas are no good? Absolutely not. It means that when you revise, you should use the suggestions in this chapter to better organize your writing.

USE TOPIC SENTENCES

A **topic sentence** presents the main idea of a paragraph. All the details in a paragraph must relate clearly and directly to that topic sentence (see page 13). If your ideas seem mixed up, check that you are using topic sentences to focus your body paragraphs. If you are not, add them. Then make sure that every sentence in each body paragraph relates to that topic sentence. If something does not relate directly, delete it or move it to another paragraph where it fits better.

WRITE A POSTDRAFT OUTLINE

You can outline your draft *after* it is written to check the organization. To do this, fill in an outline map, outline tree, outline worksheet, or formal outline with the ideas already written in your draft. (See Chapter 3.) If you discover points that do not fit logically into a particular section of the outline, you have an organization problem that needs your attention.

✳ USE TRANSITIONS

Transitions are words and phrases that show how ideas relate to each other. Sometimes when your ideas seem mixed up, you just need to supply appropriate transitions to make the connections between points explicit. Consider these sentences:

> Today's economy is not good for the stock market. There is still money to be made in speculative stocks.

Without a transitional word or phrase, the reader will not see how the ideas in the two sentences relate to each other. Add a transition, to solve this problem:

> Today's economy is not good for the stock market. <u>Nevertheless,</u> there is still money to be made in speculative stocks.

The following transitions can help you demonstrate how your ideas relate to each other:

also	later	however	in like fashion
and	earlier	on the contrary	consequently
in addition	at the same time	on the other hand	as a result
furthermore	for example	yet	therefore
moreover	for instance	although	nevertheless
indeed	in other words	even though	for this reason
in fact	in short	in the same way	in summary
near	similarly	in conclusion	in front of
now	next to	then	thus

✳ REPEAT KEY WORDS

You can often show how ideas relate to each other by repeating a key word or words, like this:

> The Senate is scheduled to vote on the tax reform <u>bill</u> Wednesday. This <u>bill</u> will reduce taxes.

✳ USE SYNONYMS

You can also demonstrate how ideas relate to each other by using synonyms to repeat a key idea, like this:

> The Senate is scheduled to vote on the tax reform <u>bill</u> Wednesday. This <u>legislation</u> will reduce taxes.

Use Outline Cards

Write your thesis and each of your main ideas on a separate index card. To experiment with alternate orders, arrange and rearrange the cards until your ideas progress in the best order.

TROUBLESHOOTING WITH A COMPUTER

If your ideas seem mixed up, the computer can provide assistance.

Copy and Rearrange Your Draft

Make a copy of your draft in a new file. Then use the cut and paste functions to try your paragraphs in a new order.

Boldface Your Thesis and Topic Sentences

Check every boldfaced topic sentence against your thesis to be sure each is clearly related. Then check every sentence in your body paragraphs to be sure each is relevant to its boldfaced topic sentence. If an idea is not relevant, delete it or revise to make it relevant.

The Postdraft Outline

Save your draft. Then create a copy of the draft in a new file. Reduce this copy to an outline by identifying in each paragraph the major idea (the topic sentence) and the major supporting details; strip everything else from each paragraph (using the delete key or a block erase), leaving just the sentences that give the main ideas and major supporting details.

Next, identify your thesis sentence and write it at the top of your outline. Now use roman and arabic numbers, capital and lowercase letters to sequence the sentences following the thesis sentence into a formal outline. Study this outline and make any necessary adjustments.

Once you have made and adjusted the outline, you can place it in a window, then recall the original draft, and revise it according to the outline. Or you can print the outline and use it as a revision guide.

Use the Internet

To view an example of a formal outline, visit this site for the University of North Carolina—at Chapel Hill's Writing Center: <www.lib.jjay.cuny.edu/research/outlining.html>. For information on writing effective transitions, visit <www.unc.edu/depts/wcweb/handouts/transitions.html>.

EXAMINING A DRAFT

To appreciate the importance of transitions, consider how much clearer the underlined transitions make the final version of this excerpt from paragraph 1 of "The Uniform Solution" on page 16.

Without transitions: Because the problems are multifaceted, the solutions are likely to be complex. Many are looking to the quick fix, in this case wearing school uniforms.

Final version: Because the problems are multifaceted, the solutions are likely to be complex. <u>However</u>, many <u>still</u> are looking to the quick fix, in this case wearing school uniforms.

CHAPTER THIRTEEN

"My Draft Is Too Short."

Y OU think you have enough ideas to get under way, so you start drafting. Then you come to the end and place a period after your last sentence. You look back over your work and come to the disheartening recognition that your draft is much too short, and you have already said everything you can think of. What do you do? No, you do not throw yourself in front of a high-speed train. Instead, try one of the strategies in this chapter.

UNDERLINE MAJOR POINTS

Underline every major point in your draft. Then check to see how much you have written after each underlined point. If one underlined point is immediately followed by another underlined point, you have neglected to develop an idea. Adding supporting detail after one or more of your major points can solve your length problem. (See Chapter 6 for ways to add supporting detail.)

When you add detail, do not state the obvious or provide unrelated information, or you will be guilty of **padding**—writing useless material just to bulk up the piece. Padding irritates readers by requiring them to read unnecessary material. Assume that you are explaining how schools foster competition, rather than cooperation, in students. If you say that schools have students compete for grades, compete for positions on sports teams, compete for student government, compete for scholarships, and compete for cheerleading, you would be providing helpful examples to illustrate your point. However, if you give a dictionary definition of *competition* as "the act of struggling to win some prize, honor, or advantage," you would be padding your essay with information your reader already knows.

✳Show after You Tell

If your draft is too short, you may be *telling* your reader things are true without *showing* that they are true. Remember to "show; don't just tell." Consider the following:

> I have always hated winter. For one thing, the cold bothers me. For another, daily living becomes too difficult.

The previous sentences are an example of telling without showing. Here is a revision with detail added to *show:*

> I have always hated winter. For one thing, the cold bothers me. Even in the house with the furnace running, I can never seem to get warm. I wear a turtleneck under a heavy wool sweater and drink one cup of hot tea after another in a futile effort to ease the chill that goes to my bones. A simple trip to the mailbox at the street leaves me chattering for an hour. My hands go numb, and my nose and ears sting from the cold. The doctor explained that I cannot tolerate the cold because I have a circulation problem which causes my capillaries to spasm, interrupting the blood flow to my extremities. I also hate winter because daily living becomes too difficult. Snow and ice are tracked into the house, necessitating frequent cleanups. Snow must be shoveled to get the car out of the driveway. Icy walks make walking treacherous, and driving to the grocery store becomes a dangerous endeavor thanks to slick, snow-covered roads.

✳Add Description

Description can add interest and liveliness, and it can help your reader form clear mental images. To flesh out an essay, look for opportunities to describe a person or scene. For more on description, see page 57.

✳Add Examples

Examples clarify matters and make things more specific. As you work to lengthen a draft, look for general statements that can be illustrated with a well-chosen example or two. For more on examples, see pages 58.

✳Add Dialogue

Sometimes you can enliven an essay by adding the words that were spoken. Consider the following paragraph:

> I stepped up to the plate, ready to swing away, but the catcher kept saying things to shake my confidence. I tried to ignore him and keep my focus, but the next

thing I knew, I was too nervous to swing at all. The pitcher threw three pitches; the umpire called three strikes; and I walked to the outfield feeling like a fool.

Notice, now, how much more full-bodied the paragraph is with the addition of dialogue:

I stepped up to the plate, ready to swing away, but the catcher kept saying things to shake my confidence. "I hope you don't choke like the last time," he sneered as I tapped the bat against the inside of my shoe. "Move in; easy out," he shouted to the outfield as I assumed my batting stance. I tried to ignore him and keep my focus, but the next thing I knew, I was too nervous to swing at all. "I figured you'd choke, you big baby," he sneered after the first called strike. The pitcher threw three pitches; the umpire called three strikes; and I walked to the outfield feeling like a fool.

EVALUATE THE SIGNIFICANCE OF AN IDEA

In addition to stating an idea, explain its importance, impact, or meaning. For example, assume you are arguing that the proposed site for the new state prison on the north end of town is not a good choice. You could explain the significance of the choice of site:

The proposed site on the north end of town is favored by state legislators, not because it is inherently the best site, but because their wealthy campaign contributors want the building as far away from their residences as possible. The legislators fear angering their wealthy supporters because they do not want to lose their financial assistance in future campaigns.

SHARE YOUR DRAFT WITH A RELIABLE READER

Ask someone with good judgment about writing to review your draft and suggest where and what kind of detail is needed. For a detailed discussion of using a reliable reader, see Chapter 11.

RETURN TO IDEA GENERATION

Your draft may be too short because you began writing before you generated enough ideas to write about. If you have a favorite idea generation technique, try it now. If it lets you down, try one or more of the other techniques described in Chapter 1.

Check Your Thesis

Study your thesis to see if it limits the territory you can cover too severely. If so, broaden the thesis a bit so that you can cover more ground and thereby increase the length of your draft. Let's say that your draft has this thesis:

> High school athletics teaches adolescents to be self-reliant.

If you have exhausted everything you can say about how high school athletics teaches self-reliance, if you have tried all the techniques in this chapter, and if you still only have a page and a half of material, consider expanding your thesis to allow discussion of other points:

> High school athletics teaches adolescents to be self-reliant. Interestingly, however, athletics also teaches young people how to be team players.

Now you can expand the draft by discussing two advantages of high school athletics rather than one.

A word of caution is in order here: Do not get carried away when you expand your thesis, or you will be forced into covering too much territory. Consider how difficult it would be to provide an adequately detailed discussion of this expanded thesis:

> High school athletics teaches adolescents everything they need to know to succeed as adults: how to be self-reliant, how to be a team player, how to function under pressure, how to accept criticism, and how to give 100 percent.

An essay with this thesis will fail in one of two ways. Either it will be so long that the reader will feel overwhelmed, or it will provide only superficial treatment of the main points.

TROUBLESHOOTING WITH A COMPUTER

The following computer strategies can help you lengthen a draft.

Separate Main Points and Supporting Details

Before each of your main points, press the insert key and hit the space bar 5 times to create a visual separation between each main point and its supporting details. The separation will help you study each point and support individually to determine if you can add an example, a story, a dialogue, or a description. After making your additions, rejoin your sentences to form a longer draft.

PRINT EACH PARAGRAPH ON A SEPARATE PAGE

Print each of your body paragraphs on a separate page and boldface each topic sentence. The separation can help you determine whether you have enough detail to back up the topic sentence.

COUNT YOUR WORDS

Many programs allow you to do a word count. If you are using MS Word, click on "Tools" and then "Word Count" to determine how close you are to the required length of the assignment. You can also highlight an individual paragraph to count its words if you like.

USE THE INTERNET

Examples are an excellent way to clarify points and add details. Visit this Capital Community College site for helpful information on using examples: <www.ccc.commnet.edu/grammar/composition/examples.htm>.

EXAMINING A DRAFT

The following is a first draft of paragraph 5 of "The Uniform Solution" on page 16. Read it and decide what kinds of details could—and should—be added. Then compare the paragraph to the final version to see what the writer added.

People who want school uniforms say that having such uniforms will save parents money because they will not have to buy expensive clothes. However, not everything should be about money. Uniforms probably are a cost saving device for parents, but the drawbacks overshadow the good aspect of the amount of money parents can save. An important drawback is the fact that students lose the freedom to express themselves through their clothing.

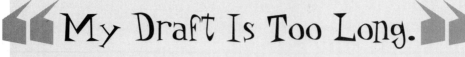

CHAPTER FOURTEEN

"My Draft Is Too Long."

Perhaps you are inspired and write page after page after page after page—all the while feeling great because you have so much to say. Unfortunately, longer is not necessarily better. Your reader's time is valuable, so keep your writing to a length that will not unduly tax your audience. If your draft is too long, try the strategies given here.

CHECK YOUR THESIS

Look for ways to narrow the scope of your thesis. If your thesis takes in too much territory, you will be forced to cover too many points, and the result will be a very long piece of writing. Consider this thesis:

> The amount of violence on television, in the movies, and in popular fiction is alarming.

To discuss television, movie, and book violence in adequate detail would require many, many pages. A more manageable piece of writing would result from a thesis like this:

> The amount of violence in prime-time network television is alarming.

ELIMINATE UNNECESSARY POINTS

Be sure you are not making unnecessary points. For example, assume you are writing a report on the mutual funds that provide the best retirement income. If you are writing for your boss, who is an investment banker, it would be silly to define the term *mutual funds*. However, in a newspaper article for readers who may not know what mutual funds are, a definition would be helpful. Similarly, if you are comparing two kinds of bicycles, you should not mention that both have two tires, as this would be stating the obvious.

❋OUTLINE YOUR DRAFT

Even if you outlined before drafting, outline your draft after you write it. Then check the outline to be sure you are not repeating points or including irrelevant detail. Be sure all your details are relevant to both the topic and the assertion expressed in your thesis. (See page 15.)

❋ELIMINATE WORDINESS

Eliminate wordiness in the following ways:

1. Eliminate repetition.

Wordy My biggest problem and concern was how to pay next month's rent. (Problem and concern are repetitious.)

Better My biggest problem was how to pay next month's rent.

Better My biggest concern was how to pay next month's rent.

2. Eliminate **deadwood** (words that add no meaning).

Deadwood	Better
the color green	green
mix together	mix
past history	past
end result	result
important essentials	essentials

Wordy I cannot concentrate unless I am alone by myself.

Better I cannot concentrate unless I am alone.

Better I cannot concentrate unless I am by myself.

3. Pare down wordy phrases.

Wordy	Better
in this day and age	now
in society today	today
being that	since
due to the fact that	because
for the purpose of	so

Wordy At this point in time, I do not think we can afford the rate increase.

Better I do not think we can afford the rate increase now.

4. Reduce the number of phrases.

Wordy The shortage <u>of skilled labor in this country</u> points to the need <u>for a greater number of vocational education programs.</u>

Better This country's skilled labor shortage points to a needed increase in vocational education programs.

5. Reduce the number of "that" clauses.

Wordy The reporters asked the senator to repeat the explanation <u>that she gave earlier.</u>

Better The reporters asked the senator to repeat her earlier explanation.

Do Not Overwrite Your Introduction or Conclusion

Check your introduction and conclusion to be sure one or both are not overly long. Remember, these parts of an essay are meant only to pave the way for your main discussion and tie things off at the end.

TROUBLESHOOTING WITH A COMPUTER

The following suggestions can help you find ways to shorten a draft.

Separate Your Sentences

Hit the enter key after each sentence to reformat your writing into a list of sentences. With your sentences listed, you may find it easier to check them for wordiness.

Count Your Words

Highlight each paragraph separately and use the word count feature to determine the number of words in each paragraph. If one paragraph is significantly longer than the others, check it for irrelevant detail.

Use the Find and Cut Functions

Use the find function to locate these unnecessary words: *very, some, quite, so.* If you judge they should be cut, do so.

Use the Internet

To learn more about wordiness and how to eliminate it, visit this Purdue Writing Center Site: <owl.english.purdue.edu>. Type "wordiness" into search box.

EXAMINING A DRAFT

To see how much bulk extra words can add to a draft, consider the early and final versions of just one sentence from paragraph 7 of "The Uniform Solution" on page 16.

Early version (32 words) I am certain that the problems that exist in our schools today mirror the same problems that are in our society at large, and it is important that we address these problems.

Final version (17 words) The problems in our schools mirror problems in the larger society, and these problems must be addressed.

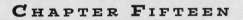

CHAPTER FIFTEEN

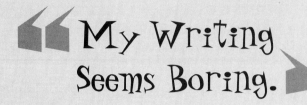

"My Writing Seems Boring."

I couldn't put it down!" "A real page-turner!" "A must read!" No, these are not the exclamations people must make about your writing, but you do have a responsibility to hold your reader's interest. If your draft seems boring, try the strategies described in this chapter to improve your detail and style.

REPLACE GENERAL WORDS WITH SPECIFIC ONES

To add interest, replace general words with more specific ones. Here are two sentences. The first has general words, which are underlined; the second has specific words, which are also underlined. Which sentence is more interesting?

General words The <u>car went</u> down the <u>street</u>.

Specific words The <u>red Corvette streaked</u> down <u>Dover Avenue</u>.

You probably found the second sentence more interesting because of its more specific word choice.

The following chart will give you a clearer idea of the difference between general and specific words.

General	Specific	General	Specific
car	1989 Buick	dog	mangy collie
sweater	yellow cardigan	hat	Phillies cap
shoes	Nike Air Max	speak	mumble
feel good	feel optimistic	book	*Angela's Ashes*
walk	saunter	drink	slurp
cry	sob loudly	said	snapped
house	two-story colonial	rain	pounding rain
a lot	twelve	later	in two days

❋ Use Active Voice

To give your writing more energy, rewrite sentences so that their subjects perform the actions indicated by the verbs. Then your sentences will be in the **active voice.** Here is an example:

> The labor leader negotiated a new contract for the autoworkers. (The action suggested by the verb <u>negotiated</u> is performed by the subject, <u>labor leader</u>.)

When the subject does not perform the verb's action (putting the sentence in the **passive voice**), the sentence has less energy:

> The new contract for the autoworkers was negotiated by the labor leader. (The subject <u>the new contract</u> does not perform the action of the verb <u>negotiated</u>.)

❋ Substitute Action Verbs for Forms of To Be

Forms of *to be (am, is, are, was, were)* have less energy and interest than action verbs, so when possible use action verbs, like this:

Less energy Mayor Daley <u>was</u> always a believer in party politics.

More energy Mayor Daley always <u>believed</u> in party politics.

❋ Rewrite Clichés

Clichés are tired, overworked expressions. At one time the expressions were fresh and interesting, but because of overuse, they have become boring. Here is a representative sampling of clichés:

cold as ice	free as a bird	sadder but wiser
high as a kite	last but not least	green with envy
fresh as a daisy	stiff as a board	hard as nails
under the weather	bull in a china shop	raining cats and dogs
in the same boat	the last straw	smart as a whip

To add interest, replace clichés with more original phrasings.

Cliché When the police officer pulled me over for speeding, I was <u>shaking like a leaf.</u>

Revision When the police officer pulled me over for speeding, I was trembling with anxiety.

❋ Eliminate Obvious Statements

Stating the obvious makes writing boring. Let's say that you are arguing that young people should not be permitted to watch more than an hour of television a day. A sentence like the following will bore a reader because some of what it says is so obvious it does not need to be said at all.

Television, an electronic device for bringing sound and pictures into the home, can be a positive or negative influence on our children, depending on how it is used.

To make your writing more interesting, eliminate obvious statements:

Television can influence our children for good or ill, depending on how it is used.

Include Dialogue

Including the words people spoke is a good way to enliven writing, especially when you are telling a story, because dialogue adds interest and immediacy. For more on dialogue, see page 94.

Add Description

Description adds vitality and interest, so look for opportunities to describe something: a scene, a person's clothing, a facial expression, a tone of voice, the brightness of the sun, the feel of a handshake. The description need not be elaborate, nor should it distract the reader from your main point. For example, if you are telling the story of a first encounter, some description can add liveliness, like this:

The door was open and I saw Dr. Harkness hunched over his desk, his nose on the paper he was studying, his eyes squinted into slits. I knocked on the door frame to get his attention, but the barely perceptible sound was too much for him. He jerked upright, startled by the intrusion. When he saw me, he brushed wisps of white hair from his eyes, smoothed his red and blue flannel shirt, and smiled sheepishly. "How can I help you, young man?" he asked, as he lifted his bulky frame from the chair.

Add Examples

Examples add interest because they are specific. Look for opportunities to follow a general point with an example. For instance, if you say that Lee is a scatterbrain, show this by giving the example of the time Lee locked the keys in the car three times in one day.

Tell a Story

A brief story can add interest and help establish a point by serving as an example. For instance, assume you are explaining that being a student *and* a parent can get very complicated. Also assume that one point you make is that the two roles can conflict with each other. To establish this point, you could tell the story of the time your six-year-old woke up sick three hours before your history exam and you had to get her to the doctor, arrange for a baby-sitter, pick up a prescription— and still make it to class on time.

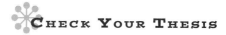

Check Your Thesis

If your thesis takes in too much territory, you can be forced into a superficial, general discussion—and such discussions are boring. For example, consider this thesis:

> *Professional sports should be reformed.*

An essay that adequately covers all professional sports and all areas that could benefit from reform is likely to involve a superficial discussion because anything in-depth will lead to a very long piece. If your thesis is too ambitious, pare it down, like this:

> *During the off-season as well as the playing season, athletes should have to submit to random drug testing.*

Now you can provide a much more interesting discussion by giving specifics and still have a piece that is a manageable length.

TROUBLESHOOTING WITH A COMPUTER

These strategies can help you improve a boring draft.

Use the Find and Replace Functions

Use the "Find" function to locate these general words: *very, quite, a lot, rather, really, great, good, bad,* and *some.* Evaluate each and decide whether to revise for more specificity.

Use the Style Check—Cautiously

If your word processing program includes a style check that flags problems, use it with caution, as these checks are not always reliable. Do not automatically assume that a flagged passage is really a problem—evaluate it yourself. Conversely, do not assume that unflagged passages are problem-free.

Use the Internet

- Purdue University Online Writing Lab has helpful information on active and passive voice. Visit it at <owl.english.purdue.edu/handouts/print/grammar/g_actpass.html>.
- For an extensive compilation of clichés given alphabetically, visit <clichesite.com>.

Sometimes writers think that passive voice sounds impressive or scholarly, so they write sentences like these from an early version of paragraph 2 of "The Uniform Solution" (page 16).

Students cannot be required by public school administrators to wear uniforms. Of course, the right to an education is guaranteed by the Constitution, so only reasonable dress codes can be put into place by public schools. If strict codes are enacted by public schools students who object to the codes for religious reasons cannot be kicked out of school.

Go back and read the opening of paragraph 2. Notice the writer changed most of the passive voice to active voice and thereby created more energetic prose.

CHAPTER SIXTEEN

"My Writing Sounds Choppy."

Read this paragraph out loud. It sounds choppy. It does not flow. The style seems immature. It sounds like it was written by someone's kid brother. This is my way of showing that choppiness is bad. Is it working?

Actually, you do not always have to read your work aloud to detect choppiness. When you read silently, the words "sound" in your brain, allowing you to "hear" this problem. Then you can eliminate it with the techniques described in this chapter.

USE DIFFERENT SENTENCE OPENERS

Writing sounds choppy when too many sentences in a row begin the same way. For example, the first paragraph of this chapter sounds choppy because most of the sentences begin with the subject. The solution is to mix the following sentence openings.

1. Open with a descriptive word (a *modifier*).

<u>Strangely</u>, little Billy did not enjoy his birthday.

<u>Confused</u>, the stranger asked directions to a bus stop.

<u>Melting</u>, the ice formed slushy puddles on the pavement.

2. Open with a descriptive phrase (a *modifier*).

<u>Despite my better judgment</u>, I bought a ticket for the roller coaster ride.

<u>Hiding in the living room</u>, twelve of us waited for the right moment to leap out and yell, "Surprise!"

<u>Pleased by her grade on the physics exam</u>, Loretta treated herself to a special dinner.

<u>Under the couch</u>, the wet dog hid from her owner.

3. Open with a *subordinate clause* (a dependent word group with a subject and verb).

<u>When Congress announced its budget reform package</u>, members of both political parties offered their support.

<u>If the basketball team can recruit a power forward</u>, we will have all the ingredients for a winning season.

<u>Before you contribute to a charity</u>, check the identification of the person requesting the money.

4. Open with *to* and the verb (an *infinitive*).

<u>To protect</u> our resources, we must all recycle.

<u>To convince</u> my parents to buy me a car, I had to agree to pay the car insurance.

<u>To gain</u> five pounds by the start of wrestling season, Luis doubled his intake of carbohydrates.

5. Open with the subject.

<u>Losses</u> led gains in today's stock market activity.

<u>Corvina's goal</u> is to become the youngest manager in the company's history.

<u>The curtains</u> were dulled by years of accumulated dirt.

✻ VARY THE PLACEMENT OF TRANSITIONS

Transitions are words and phrases that link ideas and show how they relate to each other. (Transitions are discussed on page 90.) One way to eliminate choppiness is to vary the placement of transitions.

Transition at the beginning <u>In addition</u>, providing child care in the workplace is a good idea because half of all mothers now work.

Transition in the middle Jan's opinion, <u>on the other hand</u>, is that child-care programs will cost too much.

Transition at the end Many employers now offer day care as a benefit, <u>however</u>.

✻ COMBINE SHORT SENTENCES

When you hear choppiness, look to see if you have two or more short sentences in a row. If so, combine at least two of those short sentences into a longer one, using one of these words:

and	or	for	yet
but	nor	so	because

Short sentences (choppy) The house was well constructed. It was decorated badly.

Combined sentence (smoother) The house was well constructed, but it was decorated badly.

Short sentences (choppy) The police and fire fighters both needed money. They combined their resources in a fund-raiser.

Combined sentence (smoother) The police and fire fighters both needed money, so they combined their resources in a fund-raiser.

✳ Follow Long Sentences with Short Ones and Short Sentences with Long Ones

The following examples alternate long and short sentences. As you read them, notice how well they flow.

Short followed by long The coach jumped to his feet. Although he had been coaching for 20 years, he had never before seen such a perfectly executed play.

Long followed by short This city needs a mayor who knows how to deal effectively with city council and how to trim waste from the municipal budget. This city needs Dale Davidson.

✳ Use Parallel Constructions

So sentences flow smoothly, keep series items **parallel** by putting them in the same grammatical form.

Not parallel Coach Rico values <u>teamwork</u>, <u>sportsmanship</u>, and <u>she values effort</u>.

Parallel Coach Rico values <u>teamwork</u>, <u>sportsmanship</u>, and <u>effort</u>.

Not parallel The offensive television commercial <u>insults women</u>, <u>glamorizes drinking</u>, and <u>it diminishes the importance of the family</u>.

Parallel The offensive television commercial <u>insults women</u>, <u>glamorizes drinking</u>, and <u>diminishes the importance of the family</u>.

✳ Use Your Ear

Read your writing aloud with a pen in your hand. When you hear choppiness, place a check mark. Then go back and try the techniques described in this chapter to improve the flow of sentences.

TROUBLESHOOTING WITH A COMPUTER

The following strategies can help you eliminate choppiness and improve the flow of your sentences.

USE THE STYLE CHECK—CAUTIOUSLY

Your word processing program's style check will flag parallelism problems. However, style checks are not completely reliable, so do not assume that a flagged sentence has a problem—or that an unflagged sentence is satisfactory.

USE THE COPY/MOVE FUNCTION

You can vary the placement of some transitions by copying and moving them to the beginning, middle, or end of a sentence—as needed.

Transition in the middle   The solution, <u>therefore</u>, is to start a block watch and neighborhood intervention programs.

Copy *therefore* and move it to the beginning   Therefore, the solution is to start a block watch and neighborhood interventions programs.

USE THE INTERNET

- For additional information on parallelism and transitions, visit these University of Wisconsin–Madison writing center sites:

   <www.wisc.edu/writing/Handbook/CommonErrors_Para.html> and <www.wisc.edu/writing/Handbook/Transitions.html#addition>.

- For information on sentence variety, visit this St. Cloud State site:

   <leo.stcloudstate.edu/style/sentencev.html>.

EXAMINING A DRAFT

Look again at the opening sentence from the final draft of "The Uniform Solution" (page 16). The underlined series elements are an example of parallel structure.

Right now, something is terribly wrong in our public schools: <u>test scores are down, attendance is dropping, violence is increasing, students are bored and angst-ridden, teachers are demoralized, and parents are frustrated angry, and worried</u>.

Interestingly, this sentence includes parallelism within parallelism. The second example of parallelism is underlined twice:

Right now, something is terribly wrong in our public schools: test scores are down, attendance is dropping, violence is increasing, students are bored and angst-ridden, teachers are demoralized, and parents are <u>frustrated, angry, and worried</u>.

Now read the sentence aloud to hear how the parallelism allows the sentence to flow well.

Part IV

A Troubleshooting Guide to Editing

Everyone—and I mean *everyone*—makes mistakes with grammar, spelling, punctuation, and capitalization. Frankly, there is nothing wrong with making mistakes—as long as *you* find and correct them before your *reader* does, in a process called **editing**. Editing is important because mistakes are distracting. Serious errors or frequent mistakes can also cause readers to lose confidence in your ability.

I overlook my mistakes.

Have you tried these?

- Walking away **(p. 116)**
- Listening **(p. 117)**
- Using a checklist **(p. 118)**
- Getting help **(p. 119)**

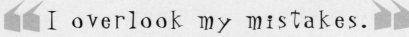 **I write fragments and run-ons.**

Have you tried these?

- Reading backwards **(p. 122)**
- Checking for warning words **(p. 123 and p. 127)**
- Studying sentences individually **(p. 127)**
- Ignoring length **(p. 128)**

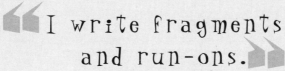 **I have trouble with pronouns.**

Have you tried these?

- Crossing out **(p. 129 and p. 130)**
- Adding words in comparisons **(p. 130)**
- Circling *who* and *whom* **(p. 132)**
- Avoiding unclear reference **(p. 133)**

I have trouble with verbs.

Have you tried these?

- Crossing out **(p. 135)**
- Rewriting questions **(p. 136)**
- Rewriting sentences with *here* and *there* **(p. 136)**
- Listening **(p. 138)**

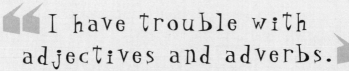

I have trouble with adjectives and adverbs.

Have you tried these?

- ❏ Distinguishing adjectives from adverbs **(p. 140)**
- ❏ Distinguishing *good* from *well* **(p. 141)**
- ❏ Checking *-ing* openers **(p. 142)**
- ❏ Moving modifiers **(p. 143)**

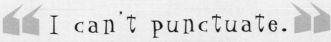

I can't punctuate.

Have you tried these?

- ❏ Checking before the subject **(p. 144)**
- ❏ Noting where a quotation occurs **(p. 148)**
- ❏ Identifying missing letters **(p. 151)**
- ❏ Using an *of* phrase **(p. 152)**

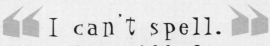

I can't spell.

Have you tried these?

- ❏ Using a spelling dictionary **(p. 158)**
- ❏ Breaking a word into parts **(p. 158)**
- ❏ Looking for prefixes **(p. 158)**
- ❏ Using memory tricks **(p. 159)**

CHAPTER SEVENTEEN

"I Don't Find My Mistakes."

When your teacher or other reader finds a mistake that you overlooked, do you smack yourself on the forehead and wonder, "How did I miss that?" You missed it because you didn't use editing strategies to help you find and correct errors. The techniques in this chapter and the ones that follow can solve that problem.

EDIT LAST

The time to **edit** (find and correct mistakes) is near the end of your writing process. During idea generation, drafting, and revising, mistakes are not an issue because you are focusing on content. If you edit during these stages, you may look up the spelling of a word that you eliminate during revision or check a comma in a sentence that never makes it to the final draft. However, once done with revising, you can scrutinize your draft for errors.

LEAVE YOUR WORK FOR A WHILE

By the time you are ready to look for errors, you may not have a fresh enough perspective to notice mistakes. To compensate for this, you should leave your writing for a day to clear your head. When you return, you will have a sharper eye for spotting errors.

POINT TO EACH WORD AND PUNCTUATION MARK

Go over your writing very slowly. If you build up even a little speed, you can overlook errors because you will see what you *intended* to write rather than what you actually *did* write. You know so well what you want to say that you may see it on the page whether it is there or not. One way to ensure that you move slowly is to point to each word and punctuation mark and study each one a second or two. Read what you are pointing to; do not move your finger or pen ahead of what you are reading, or you will build up speed and miss mistakes.

Use a Ruler

Place a ruler under the first line of your writing and examine that line for mistakes one word at a time. Then drop the ruler down a line and examine that line for mistakes. This way, you may have better luck finding errors for two reasons. First, you are less likely to build up speed and miss mistakes. Second, the ruler prevents the words below the line from entering your visual field and distracting you.

Prepare a Fresh, Word-Processed Copy

Because handwriting can be hard on the eyes, errors can be spotted more easily in type. Also, you can be more objective about word-processed copy because it seems more like printed materials—more like someone else's writing.

Listen to Your Draft

Sometimes you can hear mistakes that you overlook visually. Have someone read your draft to you, read it aloud to yourself, or speak it into a tape recorder and play back the tape. If you read your draft to yourself or into a tape recorder, be sure to read *exactly* what is on the page. Remember, writers tend to read what they *meant* to say rather than what they *did* say. Also, remember that some mistakes, such as certain misspellings, cannot be heard, so listening should be combined with visual editing.

Learn Your Pattern of Error

We all make mistakes, but we do not all make the *same* mistakes. One person may misspell words often, another may write run-on sentences, another may have trouble choosing the correct verb, and so on. Know the kinds of mistakes you make so you can make a special effort to locate those errors.

Once you know the kinds of mistakes you make, you may also determine under what circumstances you make them. For example, once you discover that you have trouble choosing verbs, a little study of your writing may tell you that you have this trouble whenever you begin a sentence with *there is* or *there are*. This is valuable information because it tells you to check the verbs in any sentences that begin with these words.

Use an Editing Checklist

An editing checklist can ensure that you are attending to everything. Use the one below or devise your own checklist of errors you habitually make.

NOTE: The page numbers in parentheses refer to helpful pages in the book.

1. Have you read your work aloud to listen for problems? (page 117)
2. Did you check every possible misspelling in a dictionary or with a spell checker? (page 157)
3. Did you edit for run-on sentences and comma splices? (page 126)
4. Did you edit for sentence fragments? (page 121)
5. Did you check your use of verbs? (page 135)
6. Did you check your use of pronouns? (page 129)
7. Did you check your use of modifiers? (page 140)
8. Have you checked any punctuation you are unsure of? (pages 144 and 148)
9. Have you checked your use of capital letters? (page 154)

Trust Your Instincts

Maybe you have had this experience: You have a feeling that something is wrong. However, you cannot give the problem a name, and you are not sure how to solve it, so you skip it and hope for the best. Then you submit your writing, and sure enough—your reader was troubled by the same thing you were troubled by. If you have had this experience, you learned that your instincts are reliable. Because much of what you know about language has been internalized, an inner alarm may sound when you have made a mistake. Always heed that alarm, even if you are not sure what the problem is or how to solve it. Get help if necessary for diagnosing and eliminating the error.

Edit More than Once

Many writers edit once for anything they can find and a separate time for each of the kinds of errors they have a tendency to make.

When in Doubt, Check It Out

When you are unsure about something, look it up in a grammar handbook. If you do not own one, check one out of your campus library or purchase one in your college bookstore.

LEARN THE RULES

You cannot edit confidently if you do not know the rules. Many people think the grammar and usage rules are understood only by English teachers, but the truth is that anyone can learn them. Invest in a grammar handbook, and each time you make an error, learn the appropriate rule.

GET HELP

Ask someone to go over your writing to find mistakes that you overlooked. Be sure, however, that the person who helps you edit is someone who knows grammar and usage rules; otherwise, you will not get reliable information. If your school has a writing center, you may be able to stop in there for reliable editing assistance. Remember, though, that the ultimate responsibility for editing is yours. You must learn and apply the rules on your own, with only backup help from others.

TROUBLESHOOTING WITH A COMPUTER

The following techniques may help you edit with your computer.

PUT YOUR EDITING CHECKLIST INTO A WINDOW

Split your screen, and place your editing checklist (either the one on page 118 or one you devise) into a window. Consult the checklist as you edit.

QUADRUPLE-SPACE YOUR TEXT

Reformat your text with four spaces between each line. This way, you can edit one line at a time with less text entering your visual field to distract you from the words you are studying.

EDIT THE SCREEN AND THE PAPER COPY

Edit twice. The first time through, edit on the screen, making the necessary changes as you go. Then print your text and edit a second time on the paper copy. Enter these changes into your file and print a fresh copy.

USE THE COMPUTER'S SEARCH FUNCTION TO LOCATE TROUBLE SPOTS

For example, if you habitually misuse semicolons and confuse *to* and *too*, find every semicolon, *to*, and *too* in your draft and check your usage.

USE YOUR COMPUTER'S GRAMMAR CHECK WITH CAUTION

It is not always correct, so evaluate its flags and suggestions and carefully edit on your own.

USE THE INTERNET

You can find many guides to grammar and usage online. Here are some good ones:

- ccc.commnet.edu/grammar
- webster.commnet.edu/sensen
- www.powa.org/editfrms.htm (This site discusses the editing process and links to pages on grammar and usage.)
- grammarlady.com (This site offers grammar information, and it gives a toll-free hotline number, so you can get answers to grammar questions.)

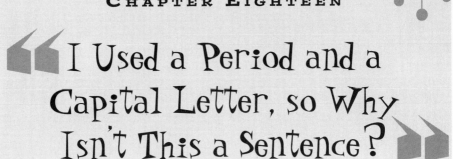

"I Used a Period and a Capital Letter, so Why Isn't This a Sentence?"

You can put a saddle on a donkey, but that won't make it a horse. Similarly, you can start a word group with a capital letter and end it with a period, question mark, or exclamation point, but that won't necessarily make it a sentence.

UNDERSTAND WHAT A SENTENCE FRAGMENT IS

If you punctuate a word group that cannot be a sentence as if it *were* a sentence, you have written a **sentence fragment.**

Word group that cannot be a sentence then fell asleep

Sentence fragment The child rolled over. <u>Then fell asleep</u>.

Correction The child rolled over. Then he fell asleep.

Word group that cannot be a sentence Although the election was close

Sentence fragment <u>Although the election was close</u>. The losing candidate did not ask for a recount.

Correction Although the election was close, the losing candidate did not ask for a recount.

Word group that cannot be a sentence such as loyalty, creativity, and integrity

Sentence fragment Maria has many admirable traits. <u>Such as loyalty, creativity, and integrity</u>.

Correction Maria has many admirable traits, such as loyalty, creativity, and integrity.

❋ Isolate Everything You Are Calling a Sentence

If your draft is relatively short, start at the beginning and place one finger of your left hand under the capital letter. Then place a finger of your right hand under the period, question mark, or exclamation point. Now read the word group between your fingers. If it sounds as if something is missing or if the word group cannot stand alone as a sentence, you probably have a sentence fragment.

Move through your entire draft this way, isolating word groups with your fingers and reading them. Each time you hear a fragment, stop and make the necessary correction.

HINT: Some people have more success if they read the word groups out loud.

❋ Read Your Draft Backward

Read your last sentence; pause for a moment to consider whether the word group can be a sentence. Then read the next-to-the-last sentence, again pausing to consider. Proceed this way until you have worked back to the first sentence.

❋ Check -*ing* and -*ed* Verb Forms

Sometimes sentence fragments result when -*ing* or -*ed* verb forms stand by themselves. Here are two examples with the -*ing* and -*ed* verb forms underlined.

Fragment The kitten <u>stretching</u> after her nap.

Fragment The child <u>frustrated</u> by the complicated toy.

To correct fragments that result when -*ing* or -*ed* verbs stand alone, pick an appropriate verb from this list and add it to the -*ing* or -*ed* form:

is   was   have   had
are   were   has

Fragment The kittens <u>stretching</u> after their naps.

Sentence The kittens <u>are stretching</u> after their naps.

Sentence The kittens <u>were stretching</u> after their naps.

Fragment The child <u>frustrated</u> by the complicated toy.

Sentence The child <u>is frustrated</u> by the complicated toy.

Sentence The child <u>was frustrated</u> by the complicated toy.

To find fragments that result when -*ing* or -*ed* verbs stand alone, go through your draft checking each -*ing* and -*ed* verb form. Read the sentence with the form and ask if a verb from the above list is necessary. Sometimes, as in the following example, an *-ed* verb *can* stand alone:

Sentence The kittens <u>stretched</u> after their naps.

✳ CHECK FOR FRAGMENT WARNING WORDS

The following words often begin sentence fragments:

after	before	such as
although	especially	unless
as	even though	until
as if	for example	when
as long as	if	whenever
as soon as	in order to	where
as though	since	wherever
because	so that	while

Check every word group that begins with one of the above words or phrases. However, do not assume that anything beginning with one of these fragment warning words is automatically a sentence fragment because sentences, too, can begin with these words and phrases. To be sure, read aloud to hear whether the words can stand alone as a sentence.

Sentence While Rudy cleaned the house, Sue cooked dinner.
Fragment While Rudy cleaned the house.

✳ WATCH OUT FOR WHO, WHOM, WHOSE, WHICH, AND WHERE

If you begin a word group with *who, whom, whose, which,* or *where* without asking a question, you most likely have written a sentence fragment.

Sentence Who lives next door?

Fragment Who lives next door.

Sentence Whose advice have I valued over the years?

Fragment Whose advice I have valued over the years.

Look at any word group that begins with *who, whom, whose, which,* or *where* and be sure that word group is asking a question. If it is not, join the word group to the sentence before it, as illustrated here:

Sentence and fragment Stavros is a good friend. <u>Whose advice I have valued over the years.</u>

Sentence Stavros is a good friend, whose advice I have valued over the years.

❋ ELIMINATE THE FRAGMENTS

The previous techniques will help you locate sentence fragments; the next two techniques will help you eliminate fragments once you find them. Keep in mind that no one technique will work for every fragment, so if one correction method does not work, try the other.

Join the Fragment to a Sentence before or after It

Sentence and fragment The custom of hat-tipping goes back to the knights. <u>Who would remove their helmets before a lord.</u>

Fragment joined to sentence The custom of hat-tipping goes back to the knights, who would remove their helmets before a lord.

Fragment and sentence <u>While trying on the cashmere sweater.</u> Molly snagged the sleeve with her class ring.

Fragment joined to sentence While trying on the cashmere sweater, Molly snagged the sleeve with her class ring.

Add the Missing Word or Words

To eliminate a fragment that results when a subject or all or part of the verb is left out, add the missing word or words.

Sentence and fragment The auto mechanic assured us the repairs would be minor. <u>Then proceeded to list a dozen things wrong with the car.</u>

Fragment eliminated with addition of the missing subject *he* The auto mechanic assured us the repairs would be minor. Then he proceeded to list a dozen things wrong with the car.

Fragment The Surgeon General announcing new nutritional guidelines.

Fragment eliminated with addition of the missing part of the verb *is* The Surgeon General is announcing new nutritional guidelines.

Sentence and fragment Police chiefs want to hire more officers. <u>However, not without additional funds.</u>

Fragment eliminated with addition of the missing subject and verb Police chiefs want to hire more officers. However, they cannot do so without additional funds.

TROUBLESHOOTING WITH A COMPUTER

You can use your computer to find and eliminate sentence fragments.

REFORMAT YOUR PAPER

Press the enter key before each capital letter that marks the start of a sentence to reformat your paper into a list of sentences. With each word group physically separated, finding fragments can be easier. When you are done with this aspect of editing, reformat your text to draw everything back together.

Use the Grammar Check—Cautiously

If your word processing program has a grammar check, it will flag sentence fragments. Although these programs do a good job of finding fragments, they are not infallible, so double check each flagged word group, and look for fragments the program might miss.

USE THE INTERNET

- The Guide to Grammar and Writing site has information on fragments, and it links to exercises you can complete for practice. Visit the site at <webster.commnet.edu/grammar/fragments.htm>.

- For information on common causes of sentence fragments, visit St. Cloud State University's site at <leo.stcloudstate.edu/punct/fragmentcauses.html>.

CHAPTER NINETEEN

"How Can This Be a Run-On or a Comma Splice? It's Not Even Long."

I f you have a tendency to write run-on sentences or comma splices, you are not alone. They are two of the most frequently occurring writing errors.

✳ UNDERSTAND WHAT RUN-ON SENTENCES AND COMMA SPLICES ARE

A **run-on sentence** occurs when two word groups that can be sentences **(independent clauses)** stand together without any separation. A **comma splice** occurs when two word groups that can be sentences (independent clauses) stand together with only a comma between them. Run-on sentences and comma splices are a problem because they blur the points where sentences begin and end.

Independent clause Charleston Harbor is a fascinating place to visit

Independent clause many historical attractions are there

A *run-on sentence* is created when these independent clauses are not separated:

Run-on sentence Charleston Harbor is a fascinating place to visit many historical attractions are there.

A *comma splice* is created when two independent clauses are separated by nothing more than a comma:

Comma splice Charleston Harbor is a fascinating place to visit, many historical attractions are there.

✳ UNDERSTAND HOW TO SEPARATE INDEPENDENT CLAUSES

You can separate independent clauses three ways.

1. **With a comma and coordinating conjunction** *(and, but, or, nor, for, so, yet)*

   Charleston Harbor is a fascinating place to visit, for many historical attractions are there.

2. **With a semicolon** (;)

   Charleston Harbor is a fascinating place to visit; many historical attractions are there.

3. **With a period and a capital letter**

   Charleston Harbor is a fascinating place to visit. Many historical attractions are there.

✳ STUDY SENTENCES INDIVIDUALLY

If your draft is not long, study each of your sentences separately. Place one finger of your left hand under the capital letter and one finger of your right hand under end mark of punctuation. Then identify the number of independent clauses (word groups that can stand as sentences) between your fingers. If you have one, the sentence is fine. If you have two or more, be sure you separate the independent clauses as explained in the previous section.

✳ UNDERLINE WARNING WORDS

Pay special attention to these words because they often begin independent clauses (word groups that can be sentences):

however	then	moreover	nevertheless
therefore	thus	furthermore	similarly
hence	finally	consequently	next
as a result	in addition	on the contrary	for example

Read over your draft and underline any of these warning words. Then check what is on *both sides* of each underlined word. If—and only if—an independent clause is on *both sides,* place a semicolon (not a comma) before the warning word.

FORGET ABOUT LONG AND SHORT

Many people think that a long sentence is sure to be a run-on or comma splice and that a short sentence cannot possibly be one. However, length is not a factor. The only factor is how independent clauses are separated.

TROUBLESHOOTING WITH A COMPUTER

The strategies that follow will help you locate run-on sentences and comma splices using computer technology.

SEARCH FOR WARNING WORDS

Use the search function to find all the run-on warning words (see above). Once these words are identified, check for independent clauses on both sides of these words. Wherever you find independent clauses on *both sides* of a warning word, be sure you have a semicolon before the word.

ISOLATE SENTENCES

Press the enter key before every capital letter marking the beginning of a sentence to reformat your paper into a list. This will make it easier to study sentences individually, following the procedure described on page 127. After finding and eliminating run-ons and comma splices, reformat your text to bring everything back together.

USE THE INTERNET

- For information on ways to correct run-on sentences, visit <owl.eed.cccoes.edu/owl/handouts/RunOn_Exp.html>.
- For information and a practice exercise, visit the City University School of New York Law School's site at <www.law.cuny.edu/wc/usage/run_on_sentences.html>.

CHAPTER TWENTY

"It Is I; It Is Me— What's the Difference?"

There you are writing along, and then it happens—you have to use a pronoun and you are not sure which one is correct: Did the police officer issue the warning to Lee and me or to Lee and I? "Lee and me; no, it's Lee and I; no, wait, Lee and me." Ah, what the heck— you pick one and hope for the best. If you stumble over pronouns, the procedures in this chapter can help.

CROSS OUT EVERYTHING IN THE PHRASE BUT THE PRONOUN

When a pronoun is joined with a noun, you may be unsure which pronoun to use. Is it "Luis and I" or "Luis and me"? Is it "the girls and us" or "the girls and we"? To decide, cross out everything in the phrase but the pronoun and read what is left:

~~My brothers and~~ I saw the movie six times.

~~My brothers and~~ me saw the movie six times.

With everything but the pronoun crossed out, you can more easily tell that the correct choice is *I:*

My brothers and I saw the movie six times.

Here is another example:

Dr. Cohen lent ~~Maria and~~ I a copy of the book.

Dr. Cohen lent ~~Maria and~~ me a copy of the book.

With everything but the pronoun crossed out, you can more easily tell that the correct choice is *me:*

Dr. Cohen lent Maria and me a copy of the book.

✳ CROSS OUT WORDS THAT RENAME

Sometimes words follow a pronoun and rename it.

We baseball players <u>Baseball players</u> follows the pronoun and renames it.

Us sophomores <u>Sophomores</u> follows the pronoun and renames it.

You sports fans <u>Sports fans</u> follows the pronoun and renames it.

To choose the correct pronoun, cross out the words that rename:

We ~~spectators~~ jumped to our feet and cheered when the band took the field.

Us ~~spectators~~ jumped to our feet and cheered when the band took the field.

With the renaming word crossed out, the correct choice is clear:

We spectators jumped to our feet and cheered when the band took the field.

Here is another example:

Loud rock music can be irritating to we ~~older folks.~~

Loud rock music can be irritating to us ~~older folks.~~

With the renaming word crossed out, the correct choice is clear:

Loud rock music can be irritating to us older folks.

✳ ADD THE MISSING WORDS IN COMPARISONS

Which is it: "Bev is a better foul shooter than I" or "Bev is a better foul shooter than me"? To find out, add the unstated word:

Bev is a better foul shooter than I am.

Bev is a better foul shooter than me am.

With the missing word added, you can tell that the correct pronoun is *I:*

Bev is a better foul shooter than I.

Here is another example:

John Grisham's new novel interested Miguel as much as I.

John Grisham's new novel interested Miguel as much as me.

To decide on the correct pronoun, add the missing words:

John Grisham's new novel interested Miguel as much as it interested I.

John Grisham's new novel interested Miguel as much as it interested me.

With the missing comparison words added, you can tell that the correct pronoun is *me.*

Use They, Their, and Them with Plural Nouns

They, their, and *them* refer to plural nouns:

All students should bring (their) notebooks to the next class; if (they) forget (them) class participation will be difficult.

A problem occurs when *they, their,* or *them* is used to refer to a singular noun:

A person who cares about the environment will recycle. (They) will also avoid using Styrofoam and plastic.

In the previous sentence the plural *they* refers to the singular *person,* creating a problem called **lack of agreement.** To eliminate the problem, make the pronoun and noun agree in one of these two ways:

Singular noun and singular pronoun A person who cares about the environment will recycle. (He or she) will also avoid using Styrofoam and plastic.

Plural noun and plural pronoun People who care about the environment will recycle. (They) will also avoid using Styrofoam and plastic.

To ensure agreement, check *they, their,* and *them* to be sure each of these pronouns refers to a plural noun. If it does not, make the noun plural or change the pronoun to a singular form.

Remember That the -Body, -One, -Thing Words Are Singular

In formal usage, *anybody, everybody, nobody, somebody, anyone, everyone, no one, someone, anything, everything, nothing, something* (the **indefinite pronouns**) are singular. Therefore, the words that refer to them should also be singular.

Everybody should remember his or her admission forms when reporting to orientation.

Someone left his or her coat in the auditorium.

Anybody who wants to bring his or her family may do so.

Be sure to put everything in its place.

Look for the indefinite pronouns. If you find one, look to see if a pronoun refers to it. If so, be sure that the pronoun is singular. Do not rely on the sound of the sentence because the plural pronoun may sound fine since it is often used in informal spoken English.

CIRCLE *WHO* AND *WHOM* AND UNDERLINE THE REST OF THE CLAUSE

To choose the correct pronoun, circle *who* or *whom* and underline the rest of the **clause** (word group with a subject and verb). If the circled word acts as a subject, use *who*. If it is the object, use *whom*. Here are some examples:

Hippocrates, ⟮who or whom?⟯ lived about 400 B.C., is called the "Father of Medicine."

Choose *who* because it is the subject of the verb *lived*.

Hippocrates, who lived about 400 B.C., is called the "Father of Medicine."

I attended the lecture by the Holocaust survivor ⟮who or whom?⟯ the community invited to speak.

Choose *whom* because it is the object of the verb *invited*.

I attended the lecture by the Holocaust survivor whom the community invited to speak.

DETERMINE *WHO* *YOU* REFERS TO

You addresses the reader. If it refers to someone other than the reader, the result is a problem called **person shift.** To avoid this problem, mentally draw an arrow from *you* to the word it refers to. If this word names someone other than the reader, replace it with the correct pronoun.

Distance runners must train religiously. ⟮You⟯ cannot compete successfully if ⟮you⟯ run only on weekends.

Now here is the corrected version;

Distance runners must train religiously. ⟮They⟯ cannot compete successfully if ⟮they⟯ run only on weekends.

CHECK *IT* AND *THEY*

Check every *it* and *they* to be sure you have supplied a noun for each of these words to refer to. Otherwise, you will have a problem called **unstated reference.**

Unstated reference Charlie is a very curious child. Because of <u>it,</u> he asks questions all the time.

Explanation *It* cannot refer to *curious* because *curious* is a modifier, not a noun. The reference is meant to be *curiosity*, but that word is not stated.

Correction Charlie is a very curious child. Because of his curiosity, he asks questions all the time.

Unstated reference   When I went to the unemployment office, <u>they</u> told me that some construction jobs were available.

Explanation   There is no stated noun for *they* to refer to.

Correction   When I went to the unemployment office, the employment counselor told me that some construction jobs were available.

AVOID UNCLEAR REFERENCE

When a pronoun can refer to more than one noun, the reader cannot tell what the writer means, creating a problem called **unclear reference.**

Unclear reference   Dad was in the garage with Brian when he heard the telephone ring.

Explanation   Because of unclear reference, the reader can't tell whether Dad or Brian heard the phone.

Correction   Dad was in the garage with Brian when Brian heard the telephone ring.

BE CAREFUL OF *THIS* AND *WHICH*

To avoid confusion, make sure that *this* and *which* refer to specific nouns.

Confusing   When people send e-mail, they expect an immediate response, whereas when they send a letter, they do not expect a quick reply. <u>This</u> interests communications specialists. (What interests communication specialists: people expecting an immediate response, people not expecting a quick reply, or the difference in expectations?)

Better   When people send e-mail, they expect an immediate response, whereas when they send a letter, they do not expect a quick reply. <u>This difference</u> interests communications specialists.

TROUBLESHOOTING WITH A COMPUTER

Your word processing program can help you edit for correct pronoun usage.

USE THE SEARCH OR FIND FUNCTION

The search or find function can help you edit efficiently.

- Find and check *they, their, them.* Be sure that these pronouns refer to plural nouns. Also be sure that *they* refers to a stated noun.

- Find and check *anybody, everybody, nobody, somebody, anyone, everyone, no one, someone, anything, everything, nothing, something.* If a pronoun refers to one of these words, be sure it is singular.

- Find and check *who* and *whom.* Subjects should be *who,* and objects should be *whom.*

- Find and check *you.* If it does not refer to the reader, change the pronoun.

- Find and check *which* and *that.* Be sure each refers to a stated noun.

USE THE INTERNET

- This University of Colorado at Colorado Springs writing center site provides links to information on many aspects of correct pronoun usage: <www.uccs.edu/~wrtgentr/handouts/pronouns.html>.

- This University of North Carolina site uses a question and answer format to give helpful information on pronouns, and it provides an exercise for practice: <www2.ncsu.edu/ncsu/grammar/Pronoun3.html>.

CHAPTER TWENTY-ONE

"How Do I Know Which Verb Form to Use?"

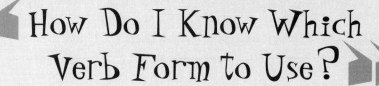

Choosing the right verb can be tricky at times, but most of the problems arise in just a few special instances. Strategies for dealing with these instances are discussed in this chapter.

CROSS OUT PHRASES BEFORE THE VERB

A phrase before the verb can trick you into choosing the wrong verb form. For example, which is correct?

The stack of books <u>is</u> about to fall.

The stack of books <u>are</u> about to fall.

To decide, cross out the phrase *of books,* and you can tell that the correct verb is *is.*

The stack ~~of books~~ is about to fall.

Phrases before the verb often begin with one of these words (called **prepositions**):

about	before	inside	over
above	between	into	through
across	by	like	to
after	during	near	toward
among	for	next	under
around	from	of	up
at	in	on	with

When in doubt about the correct verb form, cross out phrases beginning with one of these words. Here are some examples:

The container of old dishes (<u>is</u> or <u>are</u>?) on the landing.

The container ~~of old dishes~~ (<u>is</u> or <u>are</u>?) on the landing.

The container of old dishes <u>is</u> on the landing.

The herd of steers (<u>graze</u> or <u>grazes</u>?) contentedly.

The herd ~~of steers~~ (<u>graze</u> or <u>grazes</u>?) contentedly.

The herd of steers <u>grazes</u> contentedly.

The characteristics of the German sheperd (<u>make</u> or <u>makes</u>?) him a suitable show dog.

The characteristics ~~of the German sheperd~~ (<u>make</u> or <u>makes</u>?) him a suitable show dog.

The characteristics of the German shepherd <u>make</u> him a suitable show dog.

❋ REWRITE QUESTIONS

In sentences that ask questions, the verb comes before the subject. Verb choice is easier if you rewrite the sentence so it is no longer a question.

Sentence with question (<u>Have</u> or <u>has</u>?) the students finished taking exams?

Sentence rewritten The students <u>have</u> finished taking exams.

Sentence with question and correct verb <u>Have</u> the students finished taking exams?

❋ REWRITE SENTENCES BEGINNING WITH *HERE* AND *THERE*

When a sentence begins with *here* or *there*, the verb comes before the subject. When uncertain, rewrite the sentence putting the subject before the verb. The correct choice should be easier that way.

Sentence with *here* Here (<u>is</u> or <u>are</u>?) the important papers you asked for.

Sentence rewritten The important papers you asked for <u>are</u> here.

Sentence with *here* and correct verb Here <u>are</u> the important papers you asked for.

Sentence with *there* There (<u>was</u> or <u>were</u>?) an excellent dance band playing at the wedding reception.

Sentence rewritten An excellent dance band <u>was</u> playing at the wedding reception.

Sentence with *there* and correct verb There <u>was</u> an excellent dance band playing at the wedding reception.

❋ WATCH OUT FOR SUBJECTS JOINED BY *OR* AND *EITHER/OR*

Whether subjects joined by *or* and *either/or* (called **compound subjects**) take a singular or plural verb depends on what subjects are joined.

1. **If both subjects are singular, use a singular verb.**

   Joyce or Rico <u>expects</u> to pick me up for the concert.

   Either the steak or the veal roast <u>is</u> on sale at the market.

2. **If both subjects are plural, use a plural verb.**

The (boxes) or the (fishing poles) are behind the door.

Either the (scouts) or their (leaders) visit the elderly every week.

3. **If one subject is singular and the other is plural, place the plural subject second and use a plural verb.**

The (gardenia) or the (roses) make a lovely centerpiece.

Either my (sister) or my (brothers) cook Thanksgiving dinner each year.

✳ WATCH OUT FOR INDEFINITE PRONOUNS

The **indefinite pronouns** are *each, either, neither, one, none, no one, nothing, nobody, anyone, anybody, anything, everyone, everybody, everything, someone, somebody, something.* In formal usage, these indefinite pronouns take singular verbs—even though the sense of the sentence suggests a plural verb is logical. When you have used one of these words as the subject of a sentence, mentally circle the word and draw an arrow to the verb. Then check that verb to be sure it is singular.

(Each) of the students wants (not want) to have the test on Friday so the weekend is more relaxing.

(One) of the first museums was (not were) Altes Museum in Berlin.

(Either) of these vacation plans meets (not meet) your needs.

(Neither) of these paintings suits (not suit) my taste.

(None) of Lin's excuses is (not are) believable.

Do not rely on the sound of the sentence because the plural verb may sound fine, and the singular verb may sound a little off. This is because the plural verb is often used in informal speech and writing. Nonetheless, use the singular verb for strict grammatical correctness in formal usage.

✳ UNDERSTAND VERB TENSES

Tense means "time." Different verb tenses indicate different times.

1. Use the **present tense** to show the following:

Something is happening now The committee members are meeting in room 2.

Something happens regularly Each year, the summer hurricane season worries coastal residents.

Something is true indefinitely She applied to Ohio State University, which is in Columbus, Ohio.

2. Use the **past tense** to show that something took place before now:

The television series was cancelled after two episodes.

Cass left for the store before I arrived.

3. Use the **future tense** to show that something has not happened yet, but it will.

Next fall, the downtown reconstruction <u>will begin.</u>

4. Use the **present perfect tense** to show the following:

Something began in the past and continues into the present Already you <u>have painted</u> half of the kitchen.

Something began in the past and recently ended Jake <u>has</u> finally <u>finished</u> the test.

Something happened at an unspecified time in the past I <u>have visited</u> Spain twice.

5. Use the **past perfect tense** to show that something happened in the past before something else happened in the past:

Dimitri said that Sophia <u>had left</u> before I arrived.

6. Use the **future perfect tense** to indicate one future even will occur before another future event.

By the end of the year, I <u>will have completed</u> a psychology minor.

NOTE: If you are unsure how to form the various verb tenses, consult a grammar handbook

LISTEN TO YOUR VERB TENSES

Tense means time. Many verbs change their form to show different tenses (times):

Present tense (time) Today I <u>walk</u> two miles for exercise.

Past tense (time) Yesterday I <u>walked</u> two miles for exercise.

Future tense (time) Tomorrow I <u>will walk</u> two miles for exercise.

Sometimes a change in verb tense is necessary to show a change in time, but if you change tense inappropriately, you create a problem called **tense shift.**

Appropriate change in tense from present to past I recall that April Fools' Day began in France.

Problem tense shift from present to past After I <u>finish</u> my work, I <u>watched</u> a movie.

Read your draft out loud and listen to your verb tenses. If there are problem tense shifts, you are likely to hear them.

TROUBLESHOOTING WITH A COMPUTER

If you compose at the computer, you can try the following strategies to edit for verb problems.

USE THE SEARCH OR FIND FUNCTION

Use the search or find function to locate the indefinite pronouns given on page 137. If you discover some used as subjects, check to be sure the verb form is correct.

USE THE GRAMMAR CHECK—CAUTIOUSLY

If your word processing program includes a grammar check, it will flag many verb form problems. Because grammar checks are not always reliable, study each flagged verb yourself. Also, look for errors the computer does not flag.

USE THE INTERNET

For information on using the correct verb and for practice exercises, visit <http://webster.commnet.edu/grammar/sv_agr.htm>.

For information on tense shift, visit this Massachusetts Institute of Technology site at <http://web.mit.edu/writing/Writing_Process/verbtenseshifts.html>.

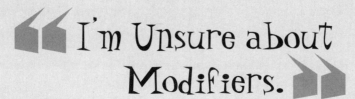

CHAPTER TWENTY-TWO

"I'm Unsure about Modifiers."

**modifier** is a word or phrase that describes. Consider this sentence:

Because of the terrible accident, traffic moved slowly.

Because *terrible* describes *accident, terrible* is a modifier; because *slowly* describes *moved, slowly* is a modifier. Modifiers take different forms in different grammatical settings. If those forms give you some trouble, the suggestions in this chapter can help.

KNOW WHEN TO USE AN ADJECTIVE AND WHEN TO USE AN ADVERB

Which sentence is correct?

The party ended so <u>abruptly</u> that no one had a chance to eat.

The party ended so <u>abrupt</u> that no one had a chance to eat.

If you are unsure, you may have trouble knowing when to use adjectives and when to use adverbs. An **adjective** describes a noun or pronoun, and an **adverb** describes a verb or other modifier. Frequently, the adverb form ends in *-ly* and the adjective form does not.

Adjectives	Adverbs
brief	briefly
swift	swiftly
loud	loudly
clear	clearly

When in doubt, mentally draw an arrow from the modifier to the word it describes. If the arrow is drawn to a noun or pronoun, use the adjective form. If the arrow is drawn to a verb or modifier, use the adverb form. Here is an example.

Diane mowed the lawn (quick or quickly?) so she could leave with her friends.

To decide, mentally draw an arrow from the modifier to the word described. If the word described is a noun or a pronoun, use the adjective; if it is a verb or another modifier, use the adverb (which often ends in -*ly*).

Diane mowed the lawn (quick or quickly?) so she could leave with her friends.

Now you can tell that *quickly* is called for because a verb is described:

Diane mowed the lawn quickly so she could leave with her friends.

Here are some more examples:

David was (absolute or absolutely?) sure of the answer.

David was absolutely sure of the answer. (A modifier is described, so the adverb is used.)

The ancient Egyptians thought of the soul as a bird that could fly around (easy or easily?).

The ancient Egyptians thought of the soul as a bird that could fly around easily. (A verb is described, so the adverb is used.)

Chris is (happy or happily?) that he was promoted after only one month on the job.

Chris is happy that he was promoted after only one month on the job. (A noun is described, so the adjective is used.)

❋ REMEMBER THAT *GOOD* IS AN ADJECTIVE AND *WELL* IS AN ADVERB—WITH ONE CAUTION AND ONE EXCEPTION

Good is an adjective; it describes nouns and pronouns:

The good news is that I got the job.

Well is an adverb; it describes verbs and modifiers:

After 10 years of lessons, Maxine plays the piano well.

Now here's the caution: After verbs like *taste, seem, appear,* and *look,* use *good* because the noun or pronoun before the verb is being described.

The meat tastes good, even though it is overcooked.

Claudia looks good, although she just had surgery.

The restaurant seems good, so let's eat here.

Now here's the exception: *Well* is used as an adjective to mean "in good health."

After six brownies and a bottle of soda, the child did not feel well.

✳ DO NOT USE MORE OR MOST WITH AN -ER OR -EST FORM

Yes: I like tacos <u>better</u> than nachos.

No: I like tacos <u>more better</u> than nachos.

Yes: The Sahara Desert is the world's <u>hottest</u> region in summer.

No: The Sahara Desert is the world's <u>most hottest</u> region in summer.

Yes: The Sahara Desert is <u>bigger</u> than the United States.

No: The Sahara Desert is <u>more bigger</u> than the United States.

Yes: The <u>rainiest</u> place on earth is Mount Waialeale, in Hawaii.

No: The <u>most rainiest</u> place on earth is Mount Waialeale, in Hawaii.

✳ CHECK SENTENCES THAT OPEN WITH -ING OR -ED VERB FORMS

An *-ing* or *-ed* verb form (called a **participle**) can be used as an adjective:

Whistling, Carolyn strolled through the park.

Whistling is a verb form that is used as an adjective to describe *Carolyn*.

Living only two or three years, lizards have a short life span.

Living is a verb form used as an adjective to describe *lizards*.

When an *-ing* or *-ed* form opens a sentence, it must be followed by the word that the form describes. Otherwise, the result will be a **dangling modifier.** Dangling modifiers can create silly sentences:

Dangling modifier While making the coffee, the toast burned.
(This sentence says that the toast made the coffee.)

Correction While making the coffee, I burned the toast. (The opening *-ing* verb form is followed by a word it can sensibly describe.)

Dangling modifier Exhausted from work, a nap was needed.
(This sentence says that the nap was exhausted.)

Correction Exhausted from work, Lucy needed a nap. (The opening *-ed* verb form is followed by a word it can sensibly describe.)

If you are in the habit of writing dangling modifiers, check every opening *-ing* and *-ed* verb form to be sure it is closely followed by a word it can sensibly describe.

Move Modifiers Near the Words They Describe

If a modifier is too far from the word it describes, the result is a **misplaced modifier.** A misplaced modifier can create a silly sentence:

Misplaced modifier Lee bought a bicycle from a neighbor with a flat tire.
    (The sentence says that the neighbor had a flat tire.)

Correction Lee bought a bicycle with a flat tire from a neighbor.
    (The modifier has been moved closer to the word it describes.)

TROUBLESHOOTING WITH A COMPUTER

If you compose at the computer, you can try the following strategies.

Use the Search or Find Function

Use the search or find function to find and check each use of *good* and *well*.

Use the Grammar Check—Cautiously

If your word processing program includes a grammar check, it will flag many errors with modifiers. However, grammar checks are not always reliable, so check each flagged error yourself, and look for errors the computer did not flag.

Use the Internet

These sites provide information on modifiers:

- <http://www.bartleby.com/64/1.html> (Click on links for adjectives, adverbs, and dangling modifiers.)
- <http://www.edufind.com/english/grammar/get_alpha.cfm?letter=A>

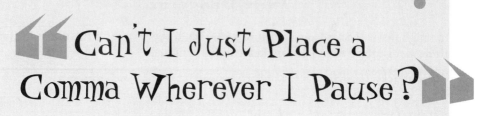

CHAPTER TWENTY-THREE

"Can't I Just Place a Comma Wherever I Pause?"

Placing commas wherever you pause is an unreliable method of punctuating: sometimes it works and sometimes it doesn't. Your best bet is to learn the rules. Editing strategies are given in this chapter to help you follow these common comma rules:

1. Use a comma after an introductory element.
2. Use a comma before a coordinating conjunction that joins independent clauses.
3. Use a comma to separate items in a series.
4. Use a comma to set off nonessential sentence elements.

For other important comma rules, consult a grammar handbook.

FIND THE SUBJECT AND LOOK IN FRONT OF IT

Most of the time, anything that comes before the subject of a sentence is an **introductory element** and should be set off with a comma. It does not matter whether the material is one word, a phrase, or a clause. Thus, once you identify the subject of a sentence, you can look in front of it. If there are any words there, follow them with a comma, like this:

Word before the subject Surprisingly, <u>the heart of a whale</u> beats only nine times a minute.

Phrase before the subject In medieval Japan, <u>fashionable women</u> blackened their teeth to enhance their appearance.

Clause before the subject Although Albert Einstein developed the theory of relativity, <u>he</u> failed his first college entrance exam.

❋FIND THE COORDINATING CONJUNCTIONS, AND THEN LOOK LEFT AND RIGHT

The following words are **coordinating conjuctions;** you can remember them by remembering *fanboys,* the word formed by the first letter of each word.

for   and   nor   but   or   yet   so

If a coordinating conjunction joins two word groups that can stand as sentences **(independent clauses),** place a comma before the conjunction.

   To apply this rule, mentally circle every coordinating conjunction; then look left and right. If an independent clause appears on both sides, place a comma before the conjunction.

                independent clause

Use comma   [I enjoy reading Stephen King novels], (but) [I do not enjoy watching
                independent clause
                horror movies.]

                independent clause

Use comma   [The Centers for Disease Control predicts a flu outbreak], (so) [I plan
                independent clause
                to get a flu shot.]

                independent clause   independent clause

Use comma   [Fish can distinguish colors], (and) [they actually prefer some colors over others.]

                                      not a clause

Do not use comma   The owl cannot move its eyes (but) [can turn its head around.]

                              not a clause

Do not use comma   The car accelerated quickly (and) [turned left.]

                              not a clause

Do not use comma   You can leave with me now (or) [wait until later.]

❋LOOK FOR SERIES

A **series** is three or more words, phrases, or clauses. Separate the items in a series with commas.

Words in a series   This restaurant specializes in <u>pasta, steak, salads,</u> and <u>seafood.</u>

Phrases in a series   Recycling centers have been established <u>at the government center,</u> <u>behind the high school,</u> and <u>at the baseball fields.</u>

Clauses in a series   <u>The manager lowered prices, the sales staff tried to be more helpful,</u> and <u>the owner remodeled the store.</u>

IDENTIFY NONESSENTIAL ELEMENTS

A **nonessential element** can be removed without changing the meaning of the sentence. Identify nonessential elements and set them off with commas. In the following sentences, the nonessential elements are underscored as a study aid.

Nonessential word The president at the time, <u>Carter,</u> worked to achieve the Egyptian-Israeli peace agreement.

Nonessential word The governor, <u>surprisingly,</u> opposed the balanced-budget amendment.

Nonessential phrase You can, <u>of course,</u> join us for dinner.

Nonessential phrase The crime rate, <u>according to the newspaper,</u> has not increased this year.

Nonessential clause Very few people understand how the election process works, <u>if you ask me.</u>

Nonessential clause Karen Carpenter, <u>who died of anorexia nervosa,</u> was a talented performer.

TROUBLESHOOTING WITH A COMPUTER

If you compose at the computer, try the following strategies to edit for commas.

USE THE DELETE KEY

If you are unsure whether an element is nonessential and, therefore, should be set off with commas, delete the element and see if necessary meaning is lost. If necessary meaning is *not* lost, use commas. After deciding, put the deleted element back in the sentence. For example, in the following sentence, is the underlined element nonessential?

Sgt. Shepherd <u>who was awarded a Purple Heart</u> is reenlisting.

Use the delete key to get

Sgt. Shepherd is reenlisting.

Because necessary meaning is not lost (we can still tell who is reenlisting), the element is nonessential. Therefore, use commas.

Sgt. Shepherd, who was awarded a Purple Heart, is reenlisting.

Here is another sentence. Is the underlined element nonessential?

The sergeant <u>who was awarded a Purple Heart</u> is reenlisting.

Use the delete key to get

The sergeant is reenlisting.

Necessary meaning is lost because we cannot tell which sergeant is reenlisting. Therefore, the element is essential and commas are not used.

The sergeant who was awarded a Purple Heart is reenlisting.

USE UNDERLINING

If you are unsure whether to use a comma before a coordinating conjunction, underline the words before and after the conjunction. Examine both sets of words. If they *both* could stand as sentence, use the comma. If neither one can be a sentence or if only one can be a sentence, do *not* use a comma.

USE THE INTERNET

Visit this page from the Guide to Writing site for an explanation of comma rules and practice exercises: <http://webster.commnet.edu/grammar/commas.htm>.

CHAPTER TWENTY-FOUR

"What If I Want to Quote Somebody?"

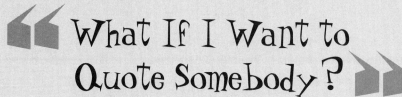

Sometimes, you want to use the words someone has spoken or written: Those words may advance a story; they may add vividness; they may lend insight into character; or they may provide support for an idea. When you quote someone, you are obligated to get it right. That means you must reproduce the words *exactly* as they were spoken or written, and it means you must follow the punctuation and capitalization rules in this chapter.

CONSIDER WHERE IN THE SENTENCE THE QUOTATION OCCURS

If your quotation comes *after* the statement of who spoke, model this form:

> Eli reminded us, "Remember to put out the campfire before retiring."

If your quotation comes *before* the statement of who spoke, model this form:

> "Remember to put out the campfire before retiring," Eli reminded us.

If your quotation comes both before and after the statement of who spoke, model the first form if the first part does *not* form a sentence. Model the second form if it does.

> "Remember," Eli reminded us, "to put out the campfire before retiring."

> "Remember to put out the campfire before retiring," Eli reminded us. "You don't want to start a forest fire."

✺ DETERMINE WHETHER THE QUOTATION OR THE ENTIRE SENTENCE ASKS A QUESTION

When the quotation asks a question, model one of these forms:

> The reporter asked Senator McEwin, "Did you vote for the trade bill?"
>
> "Did you vote for the trade bill?" the reporter asked Senator McEwin.

When the entire sentence asks a question, model this form:

> Did the newspaper really say, "The president of the school board plans to resign"?
> (The question mark appears outside the quotation mark.)

✺ REPRODUCE A PERSON'S THOUGHTS AS A QUOTATION

A person's thoughts are treated like spoken words.

> Julia thought, "It's time I made a change in my life."

✺ BE SURE YOU REALLY HAVE EXACT WORDS

Before using quotation marks, be sure you are reproducing someone's exact words.

Use quotation marks (exact words) The police officer said, "Move your car."

Do not use quotation marks (not exact words) The police officer said that you
should move your car.

 TROUBLESHOOTING WITH A COMPUTER

If you compose at the computer, consider the following strategies.

USE THE GRAMMAR CHECK—CAUTIOUSLY

If your word processing program includes a grammar check, it will flag many
misused quotation marks. However, grammar checks are not always reliable, so
check each flagged error yourself, and look for errors the computer did not flag.

USE THE INTERNET

- A convenience of using the Internet is the ability to copy and paste material from websites. However, *any* material you copy must appear in quotation marks and must be acknowledged according to the conventions explained in Chapter 29.

- For information on the uses for quotation marks not discussed in this chapter, visit Purdue University's Online Writing Lab at <http://owl.english .purdue.edu/handouts/grammar/g_quote.html>.

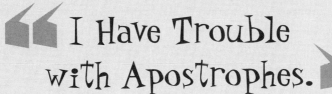

CHAPTER TWENTY-FIVE

"I Have Trouble with Apostrophes."

Apostrophes have two main functions: They take the place of missing letters in contractions, and they signal possession. Some people think apostrophes have a third function: to drive them crazy. Apostrophes *can* be pesky, so if you are unsure how to use them, try the techniques in this chapter.

IDENTIFY THE MISSING LETTER(S) IN A CONTRACTION

A **contraction** is formed by taking two words, dropping one or more letters, and joining the two words into one. In contractions, place the apostrophe at the site of the missing letter(s). For example, the contraction form of *did not* is *didn't*. Because the *o* is left out of *not*, the apostrophe is placed between the *n* and the *t*. Here are some more examples:

have + not = haven't (apostrophe at site of missing *o*)

we + will = we'll (apostrophe at site of missing *wi*)

it + is = it's (apostrophe at site of missing *i*)

NOTE: The contraction form of *will not* is the unusual *won't*.

USE IT'S ONLY WHEN YOU CAN SUBSTITUTE IT IS OR IT HAS

1. *It's* is the contraction form of *it is* or *it has*.

   It's time for a change of leadership in this state.

   (It is time for a change of leadership in this state.)

   It's been 10 years since I smoked a cigarette.

   (It has been 10 years since I smoked a cigarette.)

2. *Its* is a possessive form; it shows ownership and cannot be substituted for *it is* or *it has.*

Yes: The river overflowed <u>its</u> banks. (*Its* shows ownership.)

No: The river overflowed <u>it's</u> banks.

Yes: <u>It's</u> too late to turn back now. (*It's* here means *it is.*)

No: <u>Its</u> too late to turn back now.

❋ Avoid Contractions

No law says that you *must* use contractions. If you are unsure where to place the apostrophe, use the two-word form instead of the contraction.

❋ Use the "Of" Test

If you can add a phrase beginning with *of* to a noun or indefinite pronoun and reword, the noun or indefinite pronoun is possessive and needs an apostrophe to show that possession.

Is an apostrophe needed? The <u>books pages</u> are beginning to curl.

Add an *of* phrase The <u>pages of the book</u> are beginning to curl.

Apostrophe is needed The <u>book's pages</u> are beginning to curl.

Is an apostrophe needed? <u>Someones car</u> is parked in a no parking zone.

Add an *of* phrase <u>The car of someone</u> is parked in a no parking zone.

Apostrophe is needed <u>Someone's car</u> is parked in a no parking zone.

Is an apostrophe needed? The <u>steak knives</u> on the counter are very sharp.

Add an *of* phrase <u>The knives of steak</u> on the counter are very sharp.

No apostrophe is needed The <u>steak knives</u> on the counter are very sharp.

❋ For Possessive Forms, Ask Two Questions

Apostrophes are used with nouns to show possession. To determine how to use the apostrophe, ask, "Does the noun end in *s?*"

1. If the noun *does not* end in *s,* add an apostrophe and an *s,* like this:

President + 's = President's

The President's Council on Aging reports an increase in homelessness among the elderly.

children + 's = children's

Children's toys cost more money than they are worth.

2. If the noun *does* end in *s,* ask, "Is the noun singular or plural?"

    a. If the noun is singular, add an apostrophe and an *s,* like this:

        Delores + 's = Delores's

        Delores's new car was hit in the parking lot.

        bus + 's = bus's

        The bus's brakes jammed, causing a minor accident.

    b. If the noun is plural, add an apostrophe, like this:

        shoes + ' = shoes'

        All the shoes' laces are too long.

        mayors + ' = mayors'

        The three mayors' mutual aid agreement will yield economic benefits.

✳ WATCH OUT FOR POSSESSIVE PRONOUNS

These words are **possessive pronouns** because they show ownership: *his, hers, yours, theirs, ours,* and *its.* Since these words are already possessive, do not use them with apostrophes. (Remember that *its* is the possessive pronoun, and *it's* is the contraction form of *it is* and *it has.*)

Yes: <u>His</u> backpack was left in the car.

No: <u>His'</u> backpack was left in the car.

Yes: Are the sneakers under the couch <u>yours</u>?

No: Are the sneakers under the couch <u>your's</u>?

TROUBLESHOOTING WITH A COMPUTER

If you compose at the computer, you may like the following strategies.

USE YOUR COMPUTER'S SPELL CHECK—CAUTIOUSLY

Many programs do not check apostrophes in contractions, so misspelling such as "cant" will not be noted. Also, your spell check will not distinguish between *its* and *it's.*

USE THE INTERNET

To test how well you use apostrophes, visit this site: <http://www.agricola.umn .edu/owe/apostrophes/apostrophe.htm>. If you miss any, you can click on a link for a tutorial.

CHAPTER TWENTY-SIX

" I Never Know What to Capitalize. "

A sk people how they know what to capitalize, and many will say they aren't sure, so they just capitalize "the important stuff." Are you one of those people? If so, how do you know what's "important"? This chapter can help you use capital letters with more confidence.

CAPITALIZE THE NAMES OF ANIMALS, PEOPLE, AND THE TITLES BEFORE PEOPLE'S NAMES

Capitalize John, Lassie, Seabiscuit, Aunt Rhoda, Professor DeMatteo, Rabbi Gold

Do not capitalize boy, dog, horse, my aunt, a professor, the rabbi

NOTE: Always capitalize the pronoun *I*.

CAPITALIZE TITLES OF RELATIVES SUBSTITUTED FOR NAMES

Capitalize I bought <u>Mother and Dad</u> a DVD player for their anniversary.

Do not capitalize I bought <u>my mother and dad</u> a DVD player for their anniversary.

CAPITALIZE SPECIFIC GEOGRAPHIC LOCATIONS, NAMES OF NATIONALITIES, AND ADJECTIVES DERIVED FROM THEM

Capitalize Africa, Grand Canyon, Baltic Sea, Atlanta, Georgia, Mahoning Avenue, Stark County, Route 82, the Middle East, the Pacific Northwest, the West Coast, Chinese cooking, Irish linen

Do not capitalize continent, a canyon, sea, city, one state, the avenue, county, the northwestern region, the western part of the country

✳ Capitalize Religions, Sacred Books, and Words and Pronouns that Refer to God

Capitalize God, the Lord, Allah, the Torah, the New Testament, Muslim, Catholicism, the Holy Bible, the Trinity, Jewish, In His wisdom, God is just.

Do not capitalize the gods, a deity, a sacred text

✳ Capitalize Specific Days, Months, and Holidays

Capitalize Monday, June, Halloween

Do not capitalize day, month, holiday, winter

✳ Capitalize Specific Brand Names

Capitalize Mountain Dew, Pillsbury cake mix, Reebok tennis shoes, Cheerios, Buick

Do not capitalize soda pop, cake mix, tennis shoes, cereal, car

✳ Capitalize Specific Organizations, Companies, and Buildings

Capitalize General Motors, Disney World, Indiana University, the Empire State Building, the Fraternal Order of Police, the Red Cross

Do not capitalize car manufacturer, amusement park, college, building, fraternity, club, company

✳ Capitalize Specific Historic Events, Documents, and Periods

Capitalize the Constitution of the United States, the Battle of the Bulge, Korean War, the Magna Carta, the Renaissance

Do not capitalize a country's constitution, a battle, the war, document, historical period

CAPITALIZE TITLES CORRECTLY

Capitalize the first and last word of a title and a subtitle, no matter what those words are. In between, capitalize everything except articles *(a, an, the)*, short conjunctions *(and, but, or, nor, for, so, yet, since)*, and short prepositions *(in, on, at, of, by)*.

In the Heat of the Night   *Star Wars: The Wrath of Khan*

The Catcher in the Rye   *Making Peace with Your Past: How to Be Happy*

TROUBLESHOOTING WITH A COMPUTER

If you compose at the computer, the following strategies can help you capitalize correctly.

USE THE AUTOCORRECT FEATURE

Your word processing program may allow you to correct automatically words you routinely capitalize incorrectly. For example in Microsoft Word, use Auto-Correct by clicking on "Tools" on the tool bar and then on "Autocorrect." In the "Replace" box, type the word as you do when you capitalize it incorrectly (for example, *civil war*) In the "With" box, type the word with correct capitalization *(Civil War)*.

USE SPELL CHECK—CAUTIOUSLY

Your computer's spell check is more likely to find errors in words you have not capitalized than in words you have capitalized inappropriately.

CAPITALIZE E-MAIL CORRECTLY

In e-mail you write for school, work, or other formal and semiformal occasions, follow the capitalization rules. Using all capitals is like electronic shouting; using all lower case can be confusing.

USE THE INTERNET

- For rules for capitalization, visit this site: <http://webster.commnet.edu/grammar/capitals.htm>.
- For an exercise, visit this site: <http://webster.commnet.edu/cgi-shl/par_numberless_quiz.pl/caps_quiz.htm>.

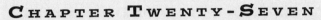
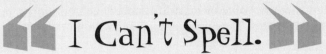

CHAPTER TWENTY-SEVEN

"I Can't Spell."

First the bad news: Misspelled words are a problem because they lead the reader to question your ability. Now the good news: Many capable people do not spell well, but they have learned ways to solve their spelling problem. You, too, can eliminate misspellings with the techniques in this chapter.

WHEN IN DOUBT, CHECK IT OUT

When it comes to using a dictionary, we all get lazy. Still, the only surefire way to check a spelling is to look up the word. If you have the slightest suspicion that a word is misspelled, check the dictionary.

BUY TWO DICTIONARIES

So looking words up is as convenient as possible, buy two dictionaries: a hardback collegiate dictionary to keep on your writing desk and a fat paperback to carry with you. You are more likely to look up a word if you have a dictionary at hand and do not have to get up and walk somewhere.

USE A PRONUNCIATION DICTIONARY

If you have trouble finding words in a traditional dictionary, try using a pronunciation dictionary that lets you find words according to the way they sound.

Use a Spelling Dictionary

Spelling dictionaries, available in most drugstores and bookstores, reference frequently misspelled words. They provide spellings without definitions, so they are thin and convenient to carry around.

Use a Pocket Spell Checker

Pocket spell checkers are electronic gadgets about the size of some calculators. They can be expensive, but if you are more inclined to check spellings with an electronic gizmo than with a dictionary, they are worth the money.

Learn Correct Pronunciations

Sometimes people misspell because they pronounce a word incorrectly. For example, you may misspell *February* if you pronounce it "Feb · u · ary"; you may misspell *preventive* if you pronounce it "pre · ven · ta · tive."

Break a Word into Parts

When a word is composed of identifiable parts, spell the word out part by part, so it is more manageable.

under · stand · able	with · hold	arm · chair
room · mate	kinder · garten	dis · ease
comfort · able	lone · liness	over · coat

Break a Word into Syllables

Some words are more easily spelled if you go syllable by syllable. Words of three or more syllables are often better handled this way.

or · gan · i · za · tion	cit · i · zen	mon · u · men · tal
Jan · u · ar · y	in · vi · ta · tion	hos · pi · tal
in · di · vis · i · ble	con · ver · sa · tion	pro · ba · bly

Look for Prefixes

When a **prefix** (word beginning) is added to a word, the spelling of the base word will usually not change.

mis · take	dis · satisfaction	mis · spell
un · nerve	un · necessary	pre · pare
mis · inform	inter · related	pre · record

Use Memory Tricks

Think of tricks to help you spell words. For example, the word *instrument* contains *strum,* and you strum a guitar, which is an instrument. Actors in a *tragedy* often *rage* at each other.

Memory tricks can be particularly helpful for pairs of words that are often mistaken for each other. You may find some of the following tricks to your liking, and you may want to make up tricks for other pairs of words that you confuse.

1. advice/advise

a. *Advice* means "a suggestion."

Joel's <u>advice</u> proved sound.

b. *Advise* means "to give advice."

Yvette is the best person to <u>advise</u> you.

MEMORY TRICK: A person with a <u>vice</u> needs ad<u>vice</u>.

2. affect/effect

a. *Affect* means "to influence."

The drought will <u>affect</u> the economy for years to come.

b. *Effect* means "result."

The <u>effects</u> of the drought are devastating.

MEMORY TRICK: The first syllable of <u>effect</u> rhymes with the first syllable of <u>result.</u>

3. among/between

a. *Among* is used for more than two.

Divide the candy <u>among</u> the four children.

b. *Between* is used for two.

The difference <u>between</u> the ages of Phil and Carlos is not important.

MEMORY TRICK: Can you fit anything <u>between</u> the <u>two e's</u> in the last syllable of <u>between?</u>

4. beside/besides

a. *Beside* means "alongside of."

I parked the van <u>beside</u> the Corvette.

b. *Besides* means "in addition to."

Besides good soil, the plants need water.

MEMORY TRICK: The final s in besides is "in addition to" the first s.

5. fewer/less

a. *Fewer* is for things that can be counted.

Fewer people voted in this election than in the last one.

b. *Less* is used for things that cannot be counted.

People who exercise regularly experience less stress than those who do not.

MEMORY TRICK: Think of countless. Less is used for things that cannot be counted.

6. then/than

a. *Then* refers to a certain time.

The trumpets blared; then the cymbals crashed.

b. *Than* is used to compare.

I like small classes better than large lectures.

MEMORY TRICK: Think of the e in then and time; think of the a in than and compare.

LEARN THE HOMOPHONES

Homophones sound alike, but they are spelled and used differently. Learn the following homophones and any others that give you trouble.

1. all ready/already

a. *All ready* means "all set."

By three o'clock, the family was all ready to leave for Virginia Beach.

b. *Already* means "by this time."

We are already an hour behind schedule, and we haven't begun the trip yet.

2. its/it's

a. *Its* shows ownership.

The car hit a pothole and broke its axle.

b. *It's* is the contraction form of "it is" or "it has."

It's too late to say you are sorry.

It's been 10 years since graduation.

3. **passed/past**

   a. *Passed* means "went by" or "handed."

   Katie <u>passed</u> the potatoes to Earvin.

   The shooting star <u>passed</u> overhead at nine o'clock.

   b. *Past* refers to previous time. It also means "by."

   I have learned from <u>past</u> experience not to trust Jerry.

   When I drove <u>past</u> the house, no one was home.

4. **principal/principle**

   a. *Principal* means "main" or "most important." It is also the school official.

   The <u>principal</u> roadblock to peace is the personalities of the country's leaders.

   The high school <u>principal</u> favors a dress code.

   b. *Principle* is a truth or standard.

   The <u>principles</u> of world economics are studied in this course.

5. **there/their/they're**

   a. *There* refers to direction or place. It is also opens sentences.

   Place the vase of flowers <u>there</u> on the coffee table.

   <u>There</u> is a surprise for you in the kitchen.

   b. *Their* shows ownership.

   The students revised <u>their</u> drafts in the computer lab.

   c. *They're* is the contraction form of "they are."

   Do not sit Lee and Dana next to each other; <u>they're</u> not getting along.

6. **threw/through**

   a. *Threw* is the past tense of *throw.*

   The shortstop <u>threw</u> the ball to the pitcher.

   b. *Through* means "in one side and out the other" or "finished."

   I had trouble getting the thread <u>through</u> the needle.

   My morning biology class is not <u>through</u> until 11:00 o'clock.

7. **to/too/two**

   a. *To* means "toward." It is also used with a verb to form the **infinitive.**

   Liza usually walks <u>to</u> school.

   Eric is learning how <u>to</u> play the violin.

b. *Too* means "excessively" or "also."

I find it <u>too</u> hot in this building.

Juanita works in the library, and she tutors math <u>too.</u>

c. *Two* is the number.

<u>Two</u> weeks ago, I bought a new car.

8. your/you're

a. *Your* shows ownership.

You left <u>your</u> keys in the car.

b. *You're* is the contraction form of "you are."

If <u>you're</u> leaving now, please take me with you.

 Underline Words to Check Later

While drafting or revising, you may sense that a word is spelled wrong. Yet looking the word up at that point is undesirable because it interrupts the drafting or revising momentum. To solve this problem, underline every word whose spelling you are unsure of as you write it. Then you have a visual reminder to look up the word later, when it is more convenient.

Keep a Spelling List

Look up the words you misspell and add the words, correctly spelled, to a list for study. Each day, study the list and memorize another word or two in an effort to increase the number of words you can spell.

TROUBLESHOOTING WITH A COMPUTER

If you compose at the computer, these tips can help you spell correctly.

Use the AutoCorrect Feature

Your word processing program may allow you to correct automatically words you routinely misspell. For example in Microsoft Word, use AutoCorrect by clicking on "Tools" on the tool bar and then on "AutoCorrect." In the "Replace" box, type the word as you do when you misspell it (for example, *defanite*) In the "With" box, type the word spelled correctly *(definitely).*

USE A SPELL CHECK—CAUTIOUSLY

Spell checks test every word you have written against the words in the dictionary in the computer's memory. If a word is not recognized, the spell check will offer alternative spellings. If the spell check comes across a typing error, it may be baffled if nothing in its memory comes close to the spelling. In this case, it will not know what to suggest as a correct spelling. Also, homophones (soundalikes) are untouched by spell checks, so the confusion of something like *there, their, they're* will not be resolved. Finally, resist the temptation to accept automatically the first spelling offered by a spell check, as it may not be the one you should use. Despite these limitations, spell checks can be helpful to people with chronic spelling problems.

USE THE INTERNET

The following sites may be helpful:

- To check spellings, you can use the Merriam-Webster online dictionary at <http://www.m-w.com>.
- For spelling rules, visit <www.gsu.edu/~wwwesl/egw/susan.htm>.
- For a list of common homonyms, visit <http://literacy.kent.edu/Midwest/Materials/ndakota/spelling/lesson1.html>.

Part V

A Troubleshooting Guide to Research

You can conduct research to draw on the words and ideas of other writers for details to include in your own writing. For example, when you write a research paper, you use multiple sources to examine a topic in depth. In fact, such a paper may include more source material than your own ideas. You can also use sources in a more limited way by including the words and ideas of other writers to support your own ideas.

Whether you are using sources in a research paper or in a shorter paper that is largely your own ideas, you must use those sources *responsibly*. This section of the book will show you how.

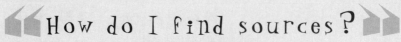

TROUBLESHOOTING STRATEGIES

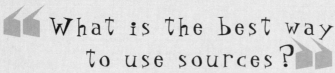

How do I find sources?

Have you tried these?

What is the best way to use sources?

Have you tried . . .

CHAPTER TWENTY-EIGHT

"How Do I Find Good Sources—and Why Do I Need Them?"

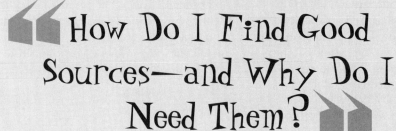

AS a writer, you don't have to "know it all"—you can get help from other writers by using sources. Here are some examples:

- In an essay arguing that juveniles who commit murder should not be tried in court as adults, you can quote a judge who says that adult courts are not set up to protect the rights of juveniles.
- In an essay explaining the benefits of a high protein diet, you can give the view of a nutritionist who believes that high protein diets are healthy.
- In an essay explaining how Internet predators work, you can summarize a newspaper account of how one such predator met children online.
- In an essay calling for an end to teacher tenure, you can give background information by looking up and explaining how, when, and why tenure became a part of American education.

This chapter will help you locate suitable sources in the library and on the Internet to use in your writing.

GET TO KNOW YOUR CAMPUS LIBRARY

Many libraries offer self-guided tours or tours conducted by librarians. Other libraries offer workshops to familiarize students with the library. Take a tour or participate in a workshop so you can work in the library efficiently.

✳ CONSIDER YOUR NEEDS

To save time and energy in the library and online, know what you're looking for. Perhaps you need a statistic to back up your observation that academic cheating is on the rise, or perhaps you want a quotation from a psychologist who believes that violent video games do not harm adolescent males. Maybe you want historical background on the nation's affirmative action laws. Knowing what you need keeps you focused.

✳ USE REFERENCE WORKS

Located in the reference section, reference works include general encyclopedias, special encyclopedias, almanacs, dictionaries, biographical dictionaries, and yearbooks. These works, which can be in paper, on CD-ROM, or on the Internet, are excellent for locating specific information, such as facts, statistics, and dates. Particularly helpful are the following:

- General subject encyclopedias such as *Encyclopedia Britannica*
- Subject encyclopedias such as *Encyclopedia of Education, Encyclopedia of Feminism,* and *Encyclopedia of Film and Television*
- *The World Almanac, Information Please Almanac,* and *Facts on File* for statistics and information on current events
- *Statistical Abstract of the United States* for information on population and American institutions
- *Current Biography* and *Webster's New Biographical Dictionary* for information on people

NOTE: For the titles of other useful reference works, speak to a librarian.

✳ USE THE COMPUTERIZED CATALOG TO LOCATE BOOKS

In the reference section, your library has a computer catalog of every book in the library. In many cases, you can also access the catalog from your own computer or sites around campus. Easy-to-follow directions should be posted near the library computers. Follow them to type in your writing topic, and books on that topic will be listed on the screen. If any of those books look helpful, write down the call number and use that number to find the book.

✳ Use Indexes to Locate Magazine, Journal, and Newspaper Articles

Magazines, journals, and newspaper articles often have the most current information. To find useful articles, look up your topic in a print, online, or CD-ROM index located in the reference room. The following indexes are a good starting point:

- *Infotrac*
- *ProQuest*
- *New York Times Index*
- *Reader's Guide to Periodical Literature*
- *ScienceSource*
- *Social Sciences and Humanities Index*
- *Academic Search Premier*
- *Lexis-Nexis*

NOTE: For the titles of other useful indexes, speak to a librarian.

✳ Search the Internet

To find useful sources online, type your topic into a **search engine,** which is a program that locates websites and web pages on whatever topic you enter into the "search" box. You may find the following search engines helpful:

www.altavista.com

www.excite.com

www.google.com

www.metacrawler.com

www.yahoo.com

Other helpful online sources include

www.refdesk.com

www.infoplease.com

www.biography.com

www.findarticles.com

www.onlinenewspapers.com

USE HIGH QUALITY SOURCES

You should evaluate each source for its reliability before using it. These guidelines can help:

- Be sure the source is recent. If your topic is General Sherman's march through Atlanta during the Civil War, a source from 1967 may be fine. However, if you are researching AIDS vaccines, a 2000 source is outdated.

- Determine whether the author has a particular bias or political leaning. A website sponsored by the National Rifle Association may not give you a balanced view of the gun control issue, and a site sponsored by Planned Parenthood may not give you a balanced view of abortion.

- Check the author's credentials. Look at book jackets, websites, and headnotes to learn about the author's publications, education, current position, and affiliations. If necessary, look up the author in a biographical dictionary.

- If you are looking at a website, determine how professional and accurate it is. Are there typos, dead links, and amateur graphics? If so, beware. Find out the site's sponsor. Sites sponsored by universities, news sources, or research foundations are usually credible. Those sponsored by hate groups, for-profit companies, and individuals with no expertise are suspect. Check when the site was last updated. Look at the links. Do they take you to credible sites?

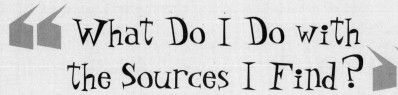

CHAPTER TWENTY-NINE

"What Do I Do with the Sources I Find?"

If you used the strategies in Chapter 28, you found sources in the library and on the Internet—maybe you even found too many sources. After all, this is the Information Age, and you may be overwhelmed by the number of sources you found. Now you need strategies for determining which sources are useful to you and which you can eliminate. Then you must determine how to use those sources that *are* helpful. This chapter can help.

✳ SKIM YOUR SOURCES TO DETERMINE THEIR USEFULNESS

To determine whether a source includes helpful information, quickly read any of the following that are available: table of contents, introduction, preface, headings, chapter titles, photo captions, charts, bold or italicized type, and summaries. For a book, read the first sentence or two of paragraphs in important chapters. For an article, read a sentence or two of each paragraph. If a particular paragraph looks promising, read all of it.

✳ PARAPHRASE IMPORTANT IDEAS

To **paraphrase,** rewrite a useful idea in *your own words and style.*

- Do not add meaning that is not in the source.
- Do not change the author's meaning.
- Do not use the author's distinctive phrasings unless you put them in quotation marks.
- Do not rewrite by going word-by-word and substituting synonyms.

Source The Bill & Melinda Gates Foundation, the richest in the country, is leading the philanthropic drive for small schools; it's committed more than $200 million to starting new ones nationwide or restructuring large high schools into smaller schools-within-a-school.

—Catherine Gewertz, "The Breakup: Suburbs Try Smaller High Schools," *Education Week*

Acceptable paraphrase According to Catherine Gewertz, the Bill & Melinda Gates Foundation has pledged over $200 million to building small high schools and also to reconfiguring existing large high schools to make them "smaller schools-within-a-school" (Gewertz).

The above paraphrase is <u>acceptable</u> because for the most part the writer expresses Gerwertz's ideas without using Gewertz's phrasings and style. When the writer *does* use Gewertz's exact words, they appear in quotation marks.

Unacceptable paraphrase According to Catherine Gewertz, the Bill & Melinda Gates Foundation, which is the wealthiest in the United States, is spearheading the charitable movement advocating small schools; the foundation has pledged more than $200 million to starting new small schools across the country or restructuring large high schools into smaller schools-within-a-school (Gewertz).

The above paraphrase is <u>unacceptable</u> because the writer merely substitutes synonyms. For example, "spearheading the charitable movement" is substituted for "leading the philanthropic drive." In addition, the writer does not use quotation marks to indicate the use of exact words, such as "restructuring large high schools into smaller schools-within-a-school."

✳ USE SUMMARY WHEN APPROPRIATE

When you want to give just the gist—the overall sense—of an author's ideas, write a **summary,** which is a highly condensed version of a source. A summary may express the ideas of several paragraphs in just a few sentences, or it may express the ideas of an entire article in just a paragraph or two. A summary restates an author's ideas in your own words and style, without changing or adding meaning.

Source the preface of this book.

Summary According to the preface, *A Troubleshooting Guide for Writers* describes strategies to help writers develop good writing processes and solve writing problems. All of the book's features work to achieve those two goals.

✳ Use Quotations Appropriately

You can quote material that is difficult to paraphrase or that is expressed in a particularly effective way. Quotations should be punctuated according to the conventions explained in Chapter 24. When you quote, retain the wording, punctuation, spelling, and capitalization in the source, with the following exceptions.

- If you need to omit a letter, word, phrase, or sentence, use three spaced periods, called **ellipsis points** (. . .) to mark the omission. If the omission comes at the end of a sentence, add a period.

Source The Bill & Melinda Gates Foundation, the richest in the country, is leading the philanthropic drive for small schools; it's committed more than $200 million to starting new ones nationwide or restructuring large high schools into smaller schools-within-a-school.

—Catherine Gewertz, "The Breakup: Suburbs Try Smaller High Schools," *Education Week*

Quotation Catherine Gewertz explains, "The Bill & Melinda Gates Foundation . . . is leading the philanthropic drive for small schools . . ." (Gewertz).

- If you need to add something to a quotation to make it fit your sentence, or if you need to add an explanation, place the addition within **brackets** ([]).

Source Circleville High School is one of 325 schools, most of them high schools, that the state has closed since 1990 in a push to consolidate small schools.

—Alan Richard, "School Merger Foes Rallying in West Virginia," *Education Week*

Quotation According to Alan Richard, "Circleville High school is one of 325 schools, most of them high schools, that the state [West Virginia] has closed since 1990 in a push to consolidate small schools" (Richard).

- If the source includes a quotation, use single quotation marks (' ') to designate this quotation within a quotation.

Source "There is too much acceptance of mediocrity," said Michael L. Ward, the tall, soft-spoken superintendent of the West Clermont Local School District, which has 9,100 students.

—Catherine Gewertz, "The Breakup: Suburbs Try Smaller High Schools," *Education Week*

Quotation Gewertz says that according to school superintendent Michael L. Ward, "'There is too much acceptance of mediocrity'" (Gewertz).

- If you introduce the quotation with *that,* do not capitalize the first word (unless it is a proper noun), and do not use a comma after the introduction.

Source The political winds around the issue may be shifting as well, with the impending retirement of a longtime legislative advocate of consolidation.

—Alan Richard, "School Merger Foes Rallying in West Virginia," *Education Week*

Quotation Alan Richard notes that "the political winds around the issue may be shifting as well, with the impending retirement of a longtime legislative advocate of consolidation" (Richard).

Quotation Alan Richard notes, "The political winds around the issue may be shifting as well, with the impending retirement of a longtime legislative advocate of consolidation" (Richard).

COMBINE SOURCES WITH EACH OTHER AND WITH YOUR IDEAS

Find ways to combine your ideas and source material to explain, support, and illustrate ideas. For example, in paragraph 2 of the sample paper on page 180, the writer combines paraphrases and quotations from Erik Nelson, Barney Berlin, and Robert Cienkus to point out the advantages of school consolidation. In paragraph 8, the writer combines his ideas with paraphrases from two sources to show that small schools have advantages, but that these advantages are offset by their drawbacks. Now is a good time to study those paragraphs.

DOCUMENT SOURCE MATERIAL APPROPRIATELY

When you paraphrase and quote, you must acknowledge that you are using other people's ideas and words, and give credit to the original writer with correct **documentation.** You can ensure proper documentation by doing the following.

Follow the Appropriate Style Sheet

A **style sheet** is a guide to how to handle source material. Papers written in the humanities, including composition, usually follow the latest edition of the *MLA Handbook for Writers of Research Papers*—often called the MLA style sheet. Papers written in many social sciences courses follow the latest edition of the *Publication Manual of the American Psychological Association*—often called APA style sheet. You can find information on these two styles sheets in your campus bookstore or online at <http://owl.english.purdue.edu/handouts/research/r_mla.html> and at <http://owl.english.purdue.edu/handouts/research/r_apa.html>. If you are unsure which style sheet to use, ask your instructor.

Introduce Source Material

Introduce each paraphrase and quotation with the author's name and a present tense verb or with a phrase like "according to." Here are examples from the paper on page 180.

- For example, according to Alan Richard,
- As Allan Ornstein reports
- Nelson goes on to note

Cite Your Source in Parentheses

If you are using the MLA style sheet, follow these guidelines:

- If the introduction to the paraphrase or quotation includes the author's name, place the page number the material came from in parentheses.
- If the introduction does not include the author's name, place both the author and page number in parentheses.
- For an online source when page numbers are not available, put the author's name in parentheses.

MLA Barney Berlin and Robert Cienkus explain that "very small districts and schools seldom have the resources—equipment, consultants, ancillary staff, curriculum variety, supplies, teaching staff—to do as good a job as larger districts" (229).

MLA Two authors explain that "very small districts and schools seldom have the resources—equipment, consultants, ancillary staff, curriculum variety, supplies, teaching staff—to do as good a job as larger districts" (Barney and Smith 229).

MLA Jim Fanning reports, "You can reduce your . . . cost by increasing the size of the [school] facility" (Fanning).

If you are using the APA style sheet, follow these guidelines:

- Place the publication date in parentheses.
- Use page numbers for quotations only—not for paraphrases.
- If you use the author's name in the introduction, place the publication date after the name. If you do not use the author's name, include it in parentheses.

APA Barney Berlin and Robert Cienkus (1989) explain that "very small districts and schools seldom have the resources—equipment, consultants, ancillary staff, curriculum variety, supplies, teaching staff—to do as good a job as larger districts" (p. 229).

APA Two authors explain that "very small districts and schools seldom have the resources—equipment, consultants, ancillary staff, curriculum variety, supplies, teaching staff—to do as good a job as larger districts" (Berlin & Cienkus, 1989, p. 229).

APA According to Nelson (1985), the strongest argument for school consolidation is that one large school is superior to multiple smaller ones because the large school can offer a greater variety of classes and extracurricular activities.

Include a List of Your Sources

For correct documentation, the last page or pages of your paper should list the sources from which you paraphrased and quoted. MLA guidelines call this list of sources the "Works Cited" page. APA guidelines call it "References." Both the works cited page and references page are an alphabetical listing according to the author's last name. If no author is given, the work is alphabetized by the first word in the title (excluding *A, An, The*). For an example of a list of sources written according to MLA guidelines, see page 182.

MLA and APA format guidelines differ for the list of references. Below are sample forms for common sources. For a complete list of forms, consult the style sheets.

Book by One Author MLA

Hillenbrand, Laura. <u>Seabiscuit: An American Legend</u>. New York: Ballantine, 2001.

Book by One Author APA

Hillenbrand, L. (2001). *Seabiscuit: An American legend*. New York: Ballantine.

Book by Two or Three Authors MLA

Hallowell, Edward M., M.D., and John J. Ratey, M.D. <u>Answers to Distraction</u>. New York: Bantam, 1996.

Book by Two or Three Authors APA

Hallowell, E.M., & Ratey, J.J. (1996). *Answers to distraction*. New York: Bantam Books.

Edition Other Than the First MLA

Zinsser, William Knowlton. <u>On Writing Well: An Informal Guide to Writing Nonfiction</u>. 5th ed. New York: Harper, 1994.

Edition Other Than the First APA

Zinsser, W.K. (1994). *On writing well: An informal guide to writing nonfiction*. (5th ed.). New York: Harper.

Book with an Editor MLA

Winokur, Jon, ed. <u>Advice to Writers: A Compendium of Quotes, Anecdotes, and Writerly Wisdom from a Dazzling Array of Literary Lights</u>. New York: Random House, 2000.

Book with an Editor APA

Winokur, J. (Ed.) (2000). *Advice to writers: A compendium of quotes, anecdotes and writerly wisdom from a dazzling array of literary lights*. New York: Random House.

Article in a Weekly Magazine MLA

Alter, Jonathan. "An Erosion of Trust." <u>Newsweek</u> 26 May 2003: 47.

Article in a Weekly Magazine APA

Alter, J. (2003, May 26). An erosion of trust. *Newsweek, 164*, 47.

Article in a Monthly Magazine MLA

"Where to Invest Now." Consumer Reports Mar 2003: 34.

Article in a Monthly Magazine APA

Where to invest now. (2003, March). *Consumer Reports,* 68, 34–38.

Article in a Scholarly Journal with Continuous Pagination through Volumes MLA

Hall, R. Mark. "The 'Oprahfication' of Literacy: Reading 'Ophrah's Book Club.'" College English 65 (2003) 646–667.

Article in a Scholarly Journal with Continuous Pagination through Volumes APA

Hall, R.M. (2003). The "Oprahfication" of literacy: Reading "Oprah's book club." *College English,* 65, 646–667.

Article in a Scholarly Journal with Separate Pagination in Each Volume MLA

Tong, T.K. "Temporary Absolutisms versus Hereditary Autocracy." Chinese Studies in History 21.3 (1988): 3–22.

Article in a Scholarly Journal with Separate Pagination in Each Volume APA

Tong, T.K. (1988). Temporary absolutisms versus hereditary autocracy. *Chinese Studies in History,* 21 (3), 3–22.

Article in a Newspaper MLA

El Nasser, Haya. "High-tech Bust Drains Bay Area Population." USA Today 10 July 2003: A1.

Article in a Newspaper APA

El Nasser, H. (2003, July 10). High-tech bust drains Bay Area population. *USA Today.* Sec. A p.1.

Online Article MLA

Fromatz, Samuel. "Groovin' with Scofield, Medeski, Martin, and Wood." All about Jazz. April 1998. 10 April 1998 <http://www.allaboutjazz.com/Bios/jxsbio.htm>.

NOTE: The first date is the publication date. The second date is the date the site was accessed.

Online Article APA

Fromatz, S. (1998, April). Groovin' with Scofield, Medeski, Martin, and Wood. *All About Jazz*. Retrieved April 10, 1998, from http://www.allaboutjazz.com/Bios/jxsbio.htm

Material from a World Wide Web Site MLA

<u>The Labyrinth: Resources for Medieval Studies</u>. Ed. Martin Irvine and Deborah Everhart. 1977. 30 April 1999 <http://www.georgetown.edu/labyrinth-home.html>.

NOTE: The second date refers to the date the site was accessed.

Material from a World Wide Web Site APA

Irvine, M. & Everhart, D. (1977). *The labyrinth: Resources for medieval studies*. Retrieved April 30, 1999 from Georgetown University: http://www.georgetown.edu/labyrinth-home.html

AVOID PLAGIARISM

Plagiarism results if you hand in all or part of another person's work as your own or if you use sources and fail to document them properly. To avoid plagiarism, which can have serious penalties, remember the following:

- Never turn in another student's work as your own, and never submit as your own all or part of a paper you have downloaded from the Internet.
- Do not copy and paste Internet material into your paper without using quotation marks or without paraphrasing it.
- Use quotation marks when you include another writer's words.
- Quote accurately, using ellipsis points and brackets as needed.
- Never add or change meaning when you paraphrase.
- Introduce source material appropriately.
- Parenthetically cite the source for every paraphrase and quotation.
- Cite every source you use on a works cited or references page.

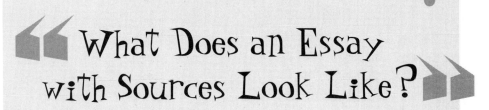

CHAPTER THIRTY

"What Does an Essay with Sources Look Like?"

I f you have never written or read an essay with sources, you may not be able to visualize such an essay or imagine yourself writing one. The following student essay, which uses sources, illustrates many of the points made in Chapters 28 and 29. These points are noted in the margins. Studying the essay, which follows the Modern Language Association style sheet explained in Chapter 29, can help you better understand how writers can incorporate source material into their writing.

Parker 1

Edmund Parker

Professor Muller

English 550

17 December 2003

The Benefits of School Consolidation

Heading

Title is centered.

paragraph 1

A. The ellipsis points are for an omission.

B. The bracket is for an addition.

C. The parenthetical citation is for an electronic source.

D. The last sentence is the thesis.

1 In response to shrinking enrollments in some districts and a steady decline in funding for education, we are seeing more and more consolidation of schools because, as Jim Fanning reports, "You can re-duce   your . . . cost by increasing the size of the [school] facility" (Fanning). Even when funding and enrollment are not an issue, some schools are combining in an effort to improve the quality of education and use tax dollars more efficiently. While school consolidation has its critics, combining schools is both practical and educationally sound.

paragraph 2

Notice the synthesis of sources.

A. The second sentence begins a paraphrase. Notice it is introduced with a present tense verb.

B. The reintroduction helps the reader know that the paraphrase continues.

C. The parenthetical citation is a page number because the author's name appears in the introduction.

D. Notice the direct quotation.

2Erik Nelson is among those who applaud the trend. He believes the strongest argument for school consolidation is that one large school is superior to multiple smaller ones because the large school can offer a greater variety of classes and extracurricular activities. He maintains that the larger enrollment makes it possible to provide a broader selection of courses, and that extracurricular offerings, including athletics, will thrive because of the merging of available monies (3). Barney Berlin and Robert Cienkus also see the advantage of consolidation. They explain that "very small districts and schools seldom have the resources—equipment, con-sultants, ancillary staff, curriculum variety, supplies, teaching staff—to do as good a job as larger districts" (229).

paragraph 3

A. The first sentence is the topic sentence.

B. Paraphrase and quotation are combined to support the topic sentence.

3 Some small school districts lack the tax base to build new schools or make necessary repairs to older buildings. For example, according to Alan Richard, Circleville High School in West Virginia had to be closed because the school desperately needed repairs and "local money wasn't an option," since the local tax base was too small to raise the needed funds (Richard).

⁴In addition to providing academic and extracurricular enrichment, consolidated schools are better able than small ones to foster the emotional and social development of students. In small schools, students have a very restricted social setting, so they have few, if any, opportunities to interact with people from different social, ethnic, racial, and religious backgrounds. Some schools are so small that the students are with the same small group of classmates from first grade through graduation.

paragraph 4

This paragraph is developed with the writer's ideas.

⁵Lack of opportunity to interact with a diverse group is not the only social problem that exists in small schools. The size can also create identity problems. In a small school, a student is so well known by peers and teachers that he or she can become trapped in a certain identity, such as "athlete," "brain," or "dummy." The identity becomes hardened in the minds of students and teachers, making it difficult for the labeled student to break out of the role and engage in different activities.

paragraph 5

This paragraph is developed with the writer's ideas.

⁶ While the small class size in small schools allows for individual attention, it can create problems for students later in college. Jane White addresses this issue. She writes that a guidance counselor at one small school feels that the adjustment from small classes to large college classes is so difficult for many students that they drop out of college (49–50).

paragraph 6

A.–B. Notice that the introduction to the paraphrase is two sentences.

⁷The benefits that consolidation provides come at a cost savings overall. According to Nelson, "Expenditures for capital improvements and basic maintenance are reduced because there is no need to upgrade or maintain duplicate facilities." Nelson goes on to note that consolidated schools require fewer administrative personnel and teachers (3). Furthermore, while a small school may not be able to afford special staff such as reading specialists, special education instructors, and media specialists, a consolidated district with its larger budget may be able to hire these important professionals.

paragraph 7

Notice that the writer's ideas are synthesized with source material.

A.–B. The quotation and paraphrase support the topic sentence.

C. This sentence expresses the writer's own thinking.

⁸Certainly small schools also have important advantages. Small class sizes mean more individual attention, but that attention does not offset lack of exposure to diverse populations. Fewer students means more pupils can find places on athletic teams and in other extracurriculars, but that benefit is offset by the fact that the number and variety of those activities are limited. In a small school, the relationship between students

paragraph 8

Note the synthesis of sources with the writer's ideas.

and teachers can be closer, and, as Allan Ornstein reports, pupils in smaller high schools tend to have higher scores on standardized tests (240). However, those benefits do not hold up in college if students in small schools tend to drop out. Furthermore, according to Catherine Gewertz, it is unclear how the size of school affects test scores because studies are inconclusive (Gewertz).

[9]Alan Richard reports the findings of the superintendent of the Pendleton County schools in West Virginia on the advantages of consolidation. While the superintendent admits that the one-on-one attention available in small schools is lost, he notes that in consolidated schools students have more advanced math classes, they are around more students their own age, and "they can join a full-size band or choir" (Richard). All in all, school consolidation is a positive trend.

paragraph 9
The conclusion provides a strong finish by citing an authority.

Works Cited

Berlin, Barney M., and Robert C. Cienkus. "Size: The Ultimate Educational Issue?" Education and Urban Society 21 (1989): 228–231.

Fanning, Jim. "Rural School Consolidation and Student Learning." ERIC Digest. Aug. 1985. 1 Dec. 2003 <http//:www.ericfacility.net/ ericdigests/ed384484.html>.

Gewertz, Catherine. "The Breakup: Suburbs Try Smaller School High Schools." Education Week. 2 May 2001. 30 Nov. 2003 <http//:www.edweek.org>.

Nelson, Erik. "School Consolidation." ERIC Digest. Washington: Office of Educational Research and Improvement, 1985. ED 282 346.

Ornstein, Allan C. "School Size and Effectiveness: Policy Implications." The Urban Review 22 (1990): 239–245.

Richard, Alan. "School Merger Foes Rallying in West Virginia." Education Week. 10 Apr. 2002. 30 Nov. 2003 <http//:www.edweek.org>.

White, Jane Robertson. "To Reorganize or Not Reorganize: A Study of Choice in a Small District." ERIC Digest. Ithaca: New York State College of Agriculture and Life Sciences at Cornell University, 1986. ED 287 627.

Part VI

Appendixes

APPENDIX A

Ideas for Writing

APPENDIX B

Taking Essay Examinations

Ideas for Writing

1. The student services division of your university plans to publish a handbook for first-year students to familiarize them with important procedures. As a student employee in student services, you have been asked to contribute to the handbook by writing an essay that explains how to do one of the following:

   a. Get a student I.D.

   b. Register for courses.

   c. Select a suitable advisor.

   d. Rush a fraternity or sorority.

   e. Manage stress.

   f. Prepare for final examinations.

   g. Find a compatible roommate.

   h. Get a parking pass.

   i. Select a major.

   When you write the essay, remember that your audience will be new students, and your purpose will be to inform them so they are better able to cope with campus life.

2. The administration of your university is concerned about drinking on your campus. You are president of student government and have been asked to help prepare an alcohol policy aimed at reducing underage drinking and at promoting responsible drinking among those of legal age who choose to drink. You can include ideas for regulations, education, disciplinary policies, and anything else you care to address. Your audience is campus administrators, and your purpose is to help develop a policy to reduce unsafe and illegal drinking practices on your campus and to persuade administrators to adopt your ideas.

3. A big birthday bash is being planned for someone you respect and care a great deal for (pick anyone you regard highly—a friend, a relative, a teacher, a coach, a member of the clergy). You have been asked to write a

character sketch of the person that presents and illustrates one or two of the person's best traits. Mention the trait or traits and go on to give examples that illustrate that trait(s). The sketch will be reprinted as a party favor. Your audience is people who also know and care for the person, and your purpose is to praise the person.

4. You are a member of the local Chamber of Commerce, which is putting together a brochure to promote tourism in your area. Pick a spot in your area (a recreational spot, a historic area, an educational place, an amusement spot) and write a description of it to be included in the brochure. Your audience is the traveler looking for a place to spend some time, and your purpose is to persuade the person to visit your area.

5. For the last week you have been home with the flu, and to pass the time you have watched television. The programming aimed at children, you have noticed, is unsatisfactory: The shows and commercials are manipulative, aimed at getting children to pester their parents for toys and sugared food. Write a letter of protest to the networks to persuade them to improve the quality of shows and commercials aimed at children.

6. When you were in high school, you were the editor of the school newspaper. Now your alma mater is planning a press day, and you have been asked to deliver a speech that expresses whether or not high school principals should be permitted to censor the contents of high school publications. Your audience will be the newspaper and yearbook staffs; your purpose will be to persuade your audience to adopt your view.

7. Congratulations! You are the winner of a writing contest. Your prize is the opportunity to have a 500- to 700-word essay published in the magazine of your choice. You may write on any topic and for any purpose. Just be sure your material is suitable for the readers of whatever magazine you choose.

8. As a guest columnist for your campus newspaper, you plan to write an article about an important campus issue: diversity, grading policies, degree requirements, extracurricular programming, or some other issue. Your audience is the campus community, and your goal is to convince readers to share your view.

9. You have recently begun an e-mail correspondence with someone who lives in another country. That person has asked you to describe American life as honestly and precisely as possible. Pick one aspect, such as shopping, dating, college life, high school, or presidential politics, and write an explanation for someone who knows very little about this country. Your purpose is to inform.

10. Pick a controversial issue and write a letter to the editor of your town newspaper expressing your view on the issue. Your audience is the readers of the newspaper, and your purpose is to persuade them to think or act in accordance with your view.

11. You are a member of the local school board. Recently, a number of parents have complained because commencement ceremonies traditionally begin with a nondenominational prayer. Although no particular religion is represented by the prayer, these parents maintain that any prayer is inappropriate because it violates the separation of church and state guaranteed by the Constitution. Furthermore, these parents maintain that the rights of atheists are violated by the prayer. Do you support the view of these parents? Write a position paper that either recommends abolishing the prayer or recommends retaining it, and support your stand. Your audience is the rest of the school board, and your purpose is to convince them to take the course of action you recommend.

12. As part of a job application, you must write a character sketch of yourself that presents and illustrates your chief strengths and weaknesses. Your audience is the personnel director, your purpose is to present a realistic yet favorable portrait.

13. If you have a job, assume that your boss has asked you to write a report that explains one change that could be made to improve efficiency, morale, or profitability. You should explain the change, why it is needed, and how it would improve operations. Your audience is your boss, your purpose is to persuade this person to institute the change.

14. In a study skills class, your instructor has assigned a paper that requires you to classify and describe the study habits of students. To research this paper, interview as many students as necessary to discover how they study, how much they study, when they study, and where they study. Your audience is your instructor, and your purpose is to inform.

15. You are taking a psychology course, and to help you appreciate how people are affected by events in their lives, your instructor has asked you to write an essay that explains how some event in your life has affected you (a death, a divorce, making a game-winning touchdown, being cut from a team, being class president, failing a test, moving to a new town, and so on). Your instructor is your audience. Your purpose is to gain insight into the effect of an event.

APPENDIX B

Taking Essay Examinations

The tips in this section can help improve your performance on essay examinations. Of course, there is no substitute for thorough studying, so the tips work only if you are prepared. If you think you need to sharpen your study skills, visit your campus study skills center.

UNDERSTAND THE VALUE OF ANXIETY

Because anxiety can keep you alert and focused so you perform well, if you are nervous before and during an exam, do not be concerned. However, while a degree of anxiety will help you, too much can make you panicky and hurt your performance. To keep your anxiety at the appropriate level, use the test-taking strategies in this appendix.

HAVE A TEST-TAKING PLAN

A plan keeps your anxiety in check because it tells you what you will do first, second, third, and so forth. When you know how you will proceed, you minimize the anxiety associated with the unknown. If you need a plan, try this:

1. Read through the entire test to understand what is expected of you.
2. Decide how you will budget your time. If you have one hour to answer four questions, plan to spend 15 minutes on each question. If some questions are worth more points than others, spend the most time on the questions worth the most points.
3. Plan your first answer with a scratch outline. Make a quick list of the points you will cover, and number them in the order you will write them up.
4. Write your first answer, using your scratch outline. Do not plan to revise; you may not have time.

5. Outline and write your next answer, and proceed in this manner until you have completed the test.

6. If you have time after answering all the questions, go back and revise as necessary.

✳ORGANIZE SIMPLY

Time is not on your side, so forget elaborate introductions and conclusions. Open with a thesis that reflects the question and go on to make your points. For example, if the question is "Explain manifest destiny," begin this way: "Manifest destiny is. . . ."

✳ANSWER THE QUESTIONS YOU ARE SURE OF FIRST

While you are answering the questions you know, a portion of your brain will turn to the ones you are less certain of, and the answers you need may occur to you.

✳THINK POSITIVELY

All things being equal, positive thinkers outperform negative thinkers.

✳PICTURE YOURSELF TAKING THE TEST

If you become overly anxious about tests, repeatedly picture yourself in the classroom, receiving the exam sheet, reading it over, writing scratch outlines, answering questions successfully, and feeling confident.

✳AVOID PADDING YOUR ANSWERS

Your instructor will recognize padding (adding unrelated information because you do not know the correct answer). A busy instructor will be annoyed by it, and you do not want to annoy the person giving you a grade.

✳IF YOU DO NOT KNOW THE ANSWER, GUESS

If you are lucky, you may get some points. Guessing is not the same as padding, however. Keep your answer to the point.

If You Run Out of Time, List the Points You Would Have Included

You may get partial credit if you demonstrate your knowledge.

Wear a Watch

You must keep track of the time so you know how long to spend on each answer.

If You Do Not Understand a Question, Ask Your Instructor for Clarification

You may not get help, but then again you may.

Index